HAMLYN
ALL COLOUR
CHINESE
COOKBOOK

HAMLYN
ALL COLOUR
CHINESE
COOKBOOK

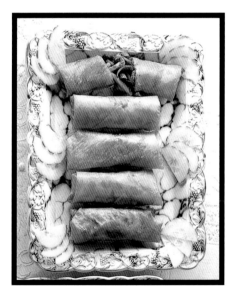

HAMLYN

Front cover shows, left to right:
Chicken in sesame sauce (recipe 77), Sesame prawn toasts (recipe 17),
Cha Shao (recipe 117)

Back cover shows, clockwise from top left:
Poached prawns with piquant dip sauce (recipe 37), Shrimp wonton soup (recipe 1),
Shanghai spring rolls (recipe 217), Peking toffee apples (recipe 225), Tomato rice (recipe 201),
Stir-fried mixed vegetables (recipe 165)

Illustrations by Gillie Newman

First published 1992 by Hamlyn.

This edition published in 1997 by Chancellor Press an imprint of
Reed International Books Ltd., Michelin House, 81 Fulham Road, London SW3 6RB
and Auckland, Melbourne, Singapore and Toronto.

Copyright © 1992 Reed International Books Limited

Some of the recipes in this book originally appeared in the Hamlyn All Colour Oriental
Cookbook, published by Reed Consumer Books in 1989.

A CIP catalogue record for this book is available from the British Library

ISBN 1 85152 846 6

Produced by Mandarin Offset
Printed and bound in China

CONTENTS

USEFUL FACTS AND FIGURES

NOTES ON METRICATION

In this book quantities are given in metric and Imperial measures. Exact conversion from Imperial to metric measures does not usually give very convenient working quantities and so the metric measures have been rounded off into units of 25 grams. The table below shows the recommended equivalents.

Ounces	*Approx g to nearest whole figure*	*Recommended conversion to nearest unit of 25*	*Ounces*	*Approx g to nearest whole figure*	*Recommended conversion to nearest unit of 25*
1	28	25	9	255	250
2	57	50	10	283	275
3	85	75	11	312	300
4	113	100	12	340	350
5	142	150	13	368	375
6	170	175	14	396	400
7	198	200	15	425	425
8	227	225	16(1lb)	454	450

Note

When converting quantities over 16 oz first add the appropriate figures in the centre column, then adjust to the nearest unit of 25. As a general guide, 1kg (1000 g) equals 2.2 lb or about 2 lb 3 oz. This method of conversion gives good results in nearly all cases, although in certain pastry and cake recipes a more accurate conversion is necessary to produce a balanced recipe.

Liquid measures

The millilitre has been used in this book and the following table gives a few examples.

Imperial	*Approx ml to nearest whole figure*	*Recommended ml*	*Imperial*	*Approx ml to nearest whole figure*	*Recommended ml*
1/4	142	150 ml	1 pint	567	600 ml
1/2	283	300 ml	1 1/2 pints	851	900 ml
3/4	425	450 ml	1 3/4 pints	992	1000 ml (1 litre)

Spoon measures

All spoon measures given in this book are level unless otherwise stated.

Can sizes

At present, cans are marked with the exact (usually to the nearest whole number) metric equivalent of the Imperial weight of the contents, so we have followed this practice when giving can sizes.

Oven temperatures

The table below gives recommended equivalents.

	°C	°F	*Gas Mark*		°C	°F	*Gas Mark*
Very cool	110	225	1/4	Moderately hot	190	375	5
	120	250	1/2		200	400	6
Cool	140	275	1	Hot	220	425	7
	150	300	2		230	450	8
Moderate	160	325	3	Very hot	240	475	9
	180	350	4				

NOTES FOR AMERICAN AND AUSTRALIAN USERS

In America the 8-fl oz measuring cup is used. In Australia metric measures are now used in conjunction with the standard 250-ml measuring cup. The Imperial pint, used in Britain and Australia, is 20 fl oz, while the American pint is 16 fl oz. It is important to remember that the Australian tablespoon differs from both the British and American tablespoons; the table below gives a comparison. The British standard tablespoon, which has been used throughout this book, holds 17.7 ml, the American 14.2 ml, and the Australian 20 ml. A teaspoon holds approximately 5 ml in all three countries.

British	*American*	*Australian*
1 teaspoon	1 teaspoon	1 teaspoon
1 tablespoon	1 tablespoon	1 tablespoon
2 tablespoons	3 tablespoons	2 tablespoons
3 1/2 tablespoons	4 tablespoons	3 tablespoons
4 tablespoons	5 tablespoons	3 1/2 tablespoons

AN IMPERIAL/AMERICAN GUIDE TO SOLID AND LIQUID MEASURES

Imperial	*American*	*Imperial*	*American*
Solid measures		Liquid measures	
1 lb butter or margarine	2 cups	1/4 pint liquid	2/3 cup liquid
1lb flour	4 cups	1/2 pint	1 1/4 cups
1 lb granulated or caster sugar	2 cups	3/4 pint	2 cups
1lb icing sugar	3 cups	1 pint	2 1/2 cups
8 oz rice	1 cup	1 1/2 pints	3 3/4 cups
		2 pints	5 cups (2 1/2 pints)

NOTE: WHEN MAKING ANY OF THE RECIPES IN THIS BOOK, ONLY FOLLOW ONE SET OF MEASURES AS THEY ARE NOT INTERCHANGEABLE.

INTRODUCTION

The cooking of China can lay claim to being one of the world's great cuisines and is certainly one of the most popular.

The HAMLYN ALL COLOUR CHINESE COOKBOOK sets out to show that there is no mystery about cooking good Chinese food. All the recipes included here are clearly presented and easy to understand. By using the right ingredients, correctly prepared, and following the straightforward method, success will be yours. The full-colour photographs accompanying each recipe serve not only to tempt your appetite and help you choose what to cook, but also to show you the finished effect you are aiming for.

To all Oriental cooks the presentation of food is of great importance, and the Chinese are no exception. Accordingly, many of the recipes shown here are attractively garnished, and instructions on making special garnishes are given in the cook's tip following each recipe where this is helpful.

The cook's tips also include a wealth of information about ingredients, whether familiar or unusual: which cut of meat to choose for a particular cooking method, for example; how to clean fish and shellfish or the quickest way to peel tomatoes. Where a dish would be enhanced by an accompanying sauce or dip, instructions on preparing it are given; where vegetables are subject to seasonal availability, alternatives are suggested. Most useful are hints about Chinese cooking methods, which along with the use of top-quality ingredients and the way different dishes are combined at one meal, provide the key to creating authentic Chinese food. The recipes in this book have been chosen to cover the most important cooking methods: steaming, simmering, braising, deep-frying and stir-frying and combinations of these, typically Chinese, known as 'crosscooking', where two methods are used in sequence to achieve delicious results.

From Soups and Snacks through Fish, Meat and Poultry to Rice, Noodles, Side Dishes and Desserts, the 236 recipes gathered here draw on dishes from all the regions of China.

The chapters in this book have been designed to help you plan a Chinese meal with ease, whether you are preparing an impressive buffet party or an informal supper. Many of the cook's tips suggest combinations of recipes, too. A look at the preparation time required will help you plan efficiently, and with a calorie count for each dish you can be sure of creating a balanced meal that is as healthy as it is delicious.

Balance and harmony, these are the watchwords of the Chinese cook, for whom every meal is a celebration. Share that pleasure with this book.

Ingredients & Seasonings

The main distinctive feature of Chinese cooking is the harmonious balance of colours, aromas, flavours and form in one dish. The relationship between these elements is reinforced by yet another feature - texture. A dish may be tender, crisp, crunchy, smooth and soft (never soggy, stringy or hard). Observing these rules when cooking is more likely to result in an authentically Chinese meal than including any number of unusual ingredients. Having said that, there are some vegetables, spices, sauces and other flavouring agents which are typically Chinese and which feature in many of the recipes in this book. Most are now widely available in supermarkets, in Chinese stores and by mail order.

The soya bean underpins Chinese cooking and deserves special mention. From it are derived a diverse range of ingredients, of which the most widely used is SOY SAUCE. This salty, thin, savoury sauce can be used in soups, stews and stir-fried dishes, as a condiment or in dips, alone or in combination. Light soy sauce is more delicate and versatile. Dark soy sauce imparts a rich colour and can be used for red-cooking, but not as a condiment. SOY BEAN PASTE is sometimes called soy bean sauce or black bean sauce. It is used in cooking instead of soy sauce when a thicker result is required. SWEET SOY BEAN PASTE or red bean sauce can be used as a dip with meat dishes or to brush on to Mandarin pancakes when serving Peking Duck. SALTED BLACK BEANS are sold in cans or polythene packs and must be soaked before use to remove excess salt. They are used in combination with other ingredients to add a distinctive flavour to stir-fried fish or meat dishes. HOISIN SAUCE is a savoury sauce based on soy beans cooked with sugar, flour, vinegar, salt, garlic, chilli and sesame seeds. Also known as barbecue sauce, it can be used as a dip or in stir-frying.

Puréed yellow soy beans are the basis for TOFU (fresh bean curd), which is sold in blocks. As a source of vegetable protein it is highly nutritious, but with little flavour of its own. For this reason it is always cooked with other ingredients. Dried bean curd is also available for use in stewed or braised dishes. FERMENTED BEAN CURD (bean curd cheese) is made by fermenting small cubes of bean curd in wine and salt. It is very salty and is used to season meat and vegetable dishes.

CEREAL PRODUCTS

RICE
There are many different types of rice grown throughout the world. For savoury Chinese dishes choose a good-quality long-grain rice such as the Indian basmati. Avoid pre-cooked or 'prefluffed' varieties. Round-grain pudding rice is best for sweet dishes.

NOODLES
Chinese noodles are usually made from durum (hard) wheat, as Italian pasta is. Dried noodles should be cooked for about 12 minutes in plenty of boiling, unsalted water and drained before use or before being incorporated in a recipe. Thread egg noodles should be immersed in boiling water, the heat turned off, and left for 4-5 minutes before draining. Cellophane noodles, beanthread noodles or mung bean threads are very fine noodles made from mung bean flour. Soak in water for 10 minutes before use. Rice stick noodles are made in southern China from rice flour. They are flat, ribbon-like strands that do not require soaking before use. They may be sold in bundles or curled up in a pad.

WONTON SKINS
Wafer-thin wrappers 7.5 cm/3 inch square made from wheat flour, egg and water. They are usually filled with a savoury mixture and then steamed, deep-fried or boiled.

VEGETABLES AND VEGETABLE PRODUCTS

AGAR-AGAR
A setting agent made from seaweed, which means that it is acceptable to vegetarians (who cannot use gelatine). Sold in powdered form or in long strands. Colourless and tasteless, it is effective without refrigeration.

BAMBOO SHOOTS
Tender young shoots from the base of the bamboo plant. The best are winter bamboo shoots, gathered at the end of the rainy season. They are parboiled before being canned, either whole or sliced.

BEAN SPROUTS
Available fresh or canned, bean sprouts are sprouted mung beans and are highly nutritious. Use fresh bean sprouts on the day of purchase. Crunchy in texture and nutty in flavour, they can be eaten raw but are usually lightly cooked.

CHILLIES
Chillies are related to capsicums (sweet peppers) but are much hotter. Fresh chillies may be red or green; dried chillies are red. Discard the seeds, which are the hottest part. When preparing fresh chillies, never touch your eyes or lips. Wash your hands immediately afterwards.

CHINESE CABBAGE
The Chinese call their cabbage *Pe-tsai*. It looks like a tightly packed cos lettuce with white midribs and can be used in salads or lightly cooked. *Pak-choi* are mustard greens, bunches of leaves which do not form a heart.

LOTUS
Various parts of this aquatic plant are used in Chinese cookery. The fresh root is sliced and eaten with a sweet sauce as a dessert. As it is only available in the west in cans, it is better used to contribute to mixed vegetable dishes. The taste is similar to globe artichoke. Lotus seeds with a slightly nutty flavour are used in vegetable dishes, soups and savoury fillings. Lotus leaves are used to wrap foods which are to be steamed, but are not themselves eaten.

MOOLI
Otherwise known as Japanese radish or *daikon*, a long, white radish with a crisp texture which may be cooked or used raw as a garnish.

MUNG BEANS
Tiny round green beans, sprouted to give bean sprouts; flour from mung beans is used to make beanthread noodles.

MUSHROOMS
Chinese mushrooms, or *shiitake*, are a beautiful pale colour when fresh, with a distinctive flavour. They are widely available in dried form and should be soaked in warm water before use. Tree ears (also called cloud ears) are fungi that grow on trees; they are sold dried, and when soaked they open out in the shape of ears. The texture is pleasantly gelatinous. Straw mushrooms — so-called because they are cultivated on beds of damp straw — are small, oval and light in colour. They are available fresh or in cans.

PICKLES
There are three main kinds of Chinese pickle. Winter pickle (salted cabbage) is brownish-green in colour, savoury and mildly salty. Snow pickle (salted mustard greens) is green in colour and has a salty flavour reminiscent of sauerkraut. Szechuan hot pickle (*Ja Chai*) is crunchy, yellow-green, hot and salty. These pickles are cooked with meat and mild vegetables and should be rinsed before use.

WATER CHESTNUT
Not a nut, but a tuber of the sedge family that grows in shallow water. Sold in cans, they are sliced for use in braised or stir-fried dishes. Though the flavour is mild, these vegetables are appreciated for their crunchy texture.

HERBS AND SPICES

CHILLI POWDER
Ground dried red chillies. Use in moderation to add pungency to savoury dishes.

CORIANDER
Fresh coriander leaves are often used as a garnish in South-east Asian cooking. It is sometimes called Chinese parsley; flat-leaved parsley is an approximate substitute. The roots are also used in Thai-influenced cooking.

FIVE SPICE POWDER
A mixture of star anise, fennel, cloves, cinnamon and Szechuan pepper, ground together.

GALANGAL
Also called laos, a root related to ginger which is used in a similar way.

GARLIC
A member of the onion family, garlic should always be used fresh. Though the odour of fresh garlic is very strong, once cooked it is much milder,and imparts a unique flavour to savoury dishes. One or two cloves are enough for most recipes.

GINGER
Fresh root ginger, sometimes called green ginger, is widely used in Chinese cooking for its pungent, aromatic qualities. Peel the knobbly, brown root before use, then slice, crush or chop it finely.

SESAME SEEDS
Used to add a nutty flavour and texture, which is accentuated if the seeds are first dry-fried.

STAR ANISE
The star-shaped seed pod of a tree belonging to the magnolia family. Gives a slightly liquorice flavour to braised and simmered dishes.

SZECHUAN PEPPER
This spice is not in fact a species of pepper, though it does have a peppery taste. It is added to cooked dishes, and served mixed with salt as a table condiment.

SAUCES, PASTES AND OILS
(see also Soya beans, above)

BLACHAN
See nam pla.

CHILLI OIL
Vegetable oil flavoured with red chillies.

CHILLI PASTE
Thickens and adds pungency to stir-fried and braised dishes. Made from chillies, soya beans, salt, sugar and flour.

CHILLI SAUCE
A very hot, reddish sauce made from red chillies. Used in cooked dishes.

CHINESE WINE
Chinese wine is made from rice and is a beautiful yellow colour. It is widely used in a range of dishes. Pale dry sherry makes a good alternative.

FISH SAUCE
See nam pla.

NAM PLA
A very salty, thin brown liquid made from fish fermented with salt and soy sauce. Anchovy essence may be used as an alternative.

OILS FOR COOKING
Peanut oil is widely used in China. This is a monounsaturated oil favoured because it adds little flavour to the food. Recommended polyunsaturated oils are sunflower, grapeseed, rapeseed and corn oils. Olive oil should not be used as the flavour is much too strong. Sesame oil, derived from sesame seeds, has a delicious, nutty flavour best appreciated when sprinkled over cooked dishes. It is not recommended for cooking as it burns easily.

OYSTER SAUCE
A dark brown sauce with a rich flavour made from oysters, salt and starch.

PLUM SAUCE
A sweet, thick sauce used in savoury braised dishes or in dips. It is available bottled.

SOUPS

Delicious as they are, most Chinese soups can be made very quickly. Some, like Shrimp wonton soup and Chicken and sweetcorn soup, are substantial and filling, while others, such as Soup with fresh greens or Fish and watercress soup, are light and elegant. All Chinese soups are appetizingly attractive to look at and highly nutritious. Home-made Chinese stock is an important basis for many soups and features in numerous other recipes in this book.

1 SHRIMP WONTON SOUP

Preparation time:
30 minutes

Cooking time:
10-15 minutes

Serves 4-6

Calories:
140-95 per portion

YOU WILL NEED:
40 sheets wonton wrappings
1.2 litres/2 pints Chinese stock
  (see recipe 2)
1 spring onion, chopped, to garnish
FOR THE FILLING
1 egg
1 teaspoon rice wine or dry sherry
salt and pepper
2 teaspoons sunflower oil
½ teaspoon sugar
1 tablespoon cornflour
225 g/8 oz prawns, peeled and chopped
100 g/4 oz fresh or canned water
  chestnuts, drained and chopped

To make the filling, mix the egg, sherry, salt, pepper, oil, sugar and cornflour in a bowl. Mix in the prawns and water chestnuts. Place ½ teaspoon filling in the centre of each wonton wrapping. Moisten the edges with water and fold into a triangle and seal. Fold again as shown in Cook's Tip below.

Heat the stock and keep it warm in a covered soup tureen.

Bring a large saucepan of water to the boil. Add the wonton a few at a time, and cook until they float to the surface. Transfer to the hot stock with a slotted spoon. Serve hot, sprinkled with the chopped spring onion.

2 CHINESE STOCK

Preparation time:
25 minutes, plus
cooling

Cooking time:
about 2½ hours

**Makes about
2.5 litres/4½ pints**

Total calories:
3573

YOU WILL NEED:
1 kg/2 lb chicken pieces
750 g/1½ lb pork spare ribs
450 g/1 lb ham, bacon or beef bones
2 teaspoons dried shrimps (optional)
50 g/2 oz fresh root ginger, unpeeled
  and roughly sliced
4-5 spring onions, trimmed
2.75 litres/5 pints water
50 ml/ 2 fl oz Chinese wine or
  dry sherry (optional)

Remove the skin from the chicken and trim off the excess fat from the pork. Place in a large saucepan with the bones, the dried shrimps (if using), the ginger and spring onions. Cover with the water and bring to the boil. Skim off the scum that rises to the surface.

Reduce the heat to a rolling boil and cook, partly covered, for at least 1½-2 hours, skimming off scum from time to time.

Leave to cool. When the stock is cold, skim any fat from the surface with a perforated spoon.

Strain the stock and return it to a clean saucepan. Add the rice wine or sherry (if using) and bring back to the boil. Simmer for 5 minutes before use.

■COOK'S TIP

Place the filling in the centre of the wrapping and fold corner to corner to make a triangle. Seal and fold the bottom corners together to form a mitre shape.

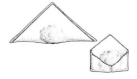

■COOK'S TIP

With the addition of seasonings, this stock can be served as a simple soup. For every 600 ml /1 pint, add 1 tablespoon light soy sauce and 1 teaspoon salt, with

2 teaspoons finely chopped spring onions. Leftover stock should be stored in a covered container in the refrigerator, where it will keep for up to 5 days.

3 MUSSEL AND BEAN CURD SOUP

Preparation time:
about 1½ hours

Cooking time:
15 minutes

Serves 4

Calories:
541 per portion

YOU WILL NEED:

1 kg/2 lb mussels, rinsed and scrubbed (see Cook's Tip)
1 tablespoon sunflower oil
2 spring onions, finely sliced
900 ml/1½ pints Chinese stock (see recipe 2)
2 cakes bean curd, cut into small dice
1 × 200 g/7 oz can straw mushrooms, drained and cut in half
2 leaves Chinese cabbage, blanched and shredded
salt and pepper
3 teaspoons cornflour
2 tablespoons water
a few drops of sesame oil, to garnish

Place the cleaned mussels in a wide pan with a little water. Cover with a lid and boil hard until the shells have opened, shaking the pan occasionally. Remove the mussels from their shells and reserve. Discard mussels that have not opened.

Heat the oil in a wok. Add the spring onions and stir-fry gently for a few seconds. Add the stock, bean curd, mussels, straw mushrooms, Chinese cabbage, salt and pepper. Simmer gently for 5 minutes. Blend the cornflour with the water and stir it into the soup to thicken it slightly.

Pour the soup into a tureen and drizzle over the sesame oil before serving.

▥ COOK'S TIP

Scrape the mussels under cold running water and scrub them clean. Pull away the beard. Discard any mussels which are broken or open.

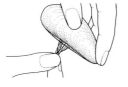

4 SOUP WITH FRESH GREENS

Preparation time:
15 minutes

Cooking time:
10-15 minutes

Serves 4

Calories:
50 per portion

YOU WILL NEED:

1.2 litres/2 pints water
1 onion, finely sliced
3 garlic cloves, sliced
3 tablespoons dried shrimps, pounded
½ teaspoon shrimp paste (optional)
2 teaspoons light soy sauce
1 teaspoon salt
225 g/8 oz fresh green leaves (watercress, sorrel, spinach or Chinese cabbage)

Put the water, onion and garlic in a large saucepan and bring to the boil. Reduce the heat, then add the shrimps, shrimp paste (if used), soy sauce and salt, stirring well. Add the green leaves.

Boil for 5 minutes, taste and adjust the seasoning. Transfer to a warmed soup tureen and serve immediately.

▥ COOK'S TIP

Shrimp paste is widely used in many Asian countries. Widely known as blachan, it is also called kapi (in Thailand) and trassi (in Malaysia). It has a very pungent smell and should be kept tightly wrapped in the refrigerator after opening. The flavour is less sharp if the paste is fried briefly before use.

5 CORN AND FISH SOUP

Preparation time:
10 minutes, plus
marinating

Cooking time:
10-12 minutes

Serves 4

Calories:
180 per portion

YOU WILL NEED:
450 g/1 lb white fish fillets
1 piece fresh root ginger, cut into
*   small dice*
1 teaspoon rice wine or dry sherry
salt
900 ml/1½ pints water
1 x 225 g/8 oz can sweetcorn, drained
1 teaspoon corn oil
1½ teaspoons cornflour
1 tablespoon water
1 spring onion, chopped, to garnish

Place the fish in a shallow heatproof dish. Squeeze the pieces of ginger in a garlic crusher to extract the juice and sprinkle it over the fish. Add the sherry and a generous pinch of salt. Leave to marinate for 10 minutes.

Place the fish in a steamer and steam for 5-6 minutes. Remove from the heat and mash the fish with a fork. Set aside.

Pour the water into a large saucepan and bring to the boil. Add the sweetcorn, oil and 1 teaspoon salt. Simmer for 2 minutes.

Mix the cornflour with the water to make a thin paste. Add to the pan and cook, stirring, until the soup thickens. Add the fish and cook for 1 minute, just to heat it through. Transfer to individual soup bowls and serve hot, sprinkled with chopped spring onion.

6 THREE SHREDDED AND FIVE INGREDIENTS SOUP

Preparation time:
10 minutes, plus
soaking

Cooking time:
20 minutes

Serves 6

Calories:
336 per portion

YOU WILL NEED:
1.5 litres/2½ pints Chinese stock
*   (see recipe 2)*
15g/ ½ oz fresh root ginger, peeled
*   and chopped*
2 garlic cloves, crushed
25 g/1 oz onion, chopped
25 g/1 oz dried shiitake mushrooms,
*   soaked for 20 minutes (see*
*   Cook's Tip)*
25 g/1 oz dried shrimps, soaked for
*   20 minutes*
2 spring onions, shredded
3 large peeled prawns, shredded
100 g/4 oz Chinese cabbage,
*   finely shredded*
1 teaspoon sesame oil, to garnish

Heat the stock in a wok or large saucepan and bring to the boil. Add the ginger, garlic and onion. Chop the mushrooms. Drain and chop the shrimps. Add the mushrooms and shrimps to the stock and simmer for 5 minutes.

Add the shredded spring onions, prawns and Chinese cabbage and simmer for a further 2 minutes.

To serve, pour into warmed soup bowls and sprinkle sesame oil on top.

■ COOK'S TIP

Cod, coley and haddock are good choices for this filling soup. As a variation, use half fresh white fish and half smoked. The golden colour of smoked cod or haddock

combines well with the sweetcorn kernels and the slight saltiness adds an interesting topnote of flavour.

■ COOK'S TIP

Soak the mushrooms in boiling water and leave to stand for 20 minutes or so, depending on size. When they are soft and plump, discard the stalks.

7   PRAWN AND SQUID HOT SOUP

Preparation time:	**YOU WILL NEED:**
20 minutes	*225 g/8 oz cleaned squid (see method)*
	1.8 litres/3 pints Chinese stock
Cooking time:	* (see recipe 2)*
10-12 minutes	*3 lime leaves*
	1 stem lemon grass, crushed
Serves 4	*225 g/8 oz uncooked prawns, peeled*
	nam pla (fish sauce), to taste
Calories:	*2-4 fresh chillies, sliced into rounds*
100 per portion	*2 garlic cloves, crushed*
	juice of 1 lime or 1 lemon
	freshly chopped coriander leaves,
	* to garnish*

To prepare the squid, hold the head and tentacles in one hand and pull away the body with the other. Pull the innards and the hard 'pen' away from the body and discard. Cut the tentacles from the head. Scrape the thin skin from the body and tentacles. Rinse well and pat dry.

Cut the squid into rings. Put the stock, lime leaves and lemon grass in a pan and bring to the boil. Reduce the heat and simmer for 5 minutes. Add the prawns, squid and nam pla. Cook until the prawns turn pink. Add the chillies.

Pour the soup into 4 warmed individual bowls. Mix together the garlic and lime or lemon juice, and stir into the soup. Sprinkle with chopped coriander and serve hot.

8   STUFFED SQUID SOUP

Preparation time:	**YOU WILL NEED:**
20 minutes	*8 medium squid*
	175 g/6 oz minced pork
Cooking time:	*1 spring onion stalk, chopped*
10 minutes	*salt and pepper*
	1 teaspoon cornflour
Serves 4	*500 ml/18 fl oz water*
	1 tablespoon light soy sauce
Calories:	*1 tablespoon sesame oil*
138 per portion	*chopped spring onions, to garnish*

Clean the squid (see recipe 7), retaining the tentacles.

Mix the minced pork with the spring onion stalk, salt, pepper and cornflour. Stuff the squid with a little of the pork mixture and secure the tentacles to each one with half a cocktail stick. Set aside any leftover stuffing mixture.

Bring the water to the boil in a large saucepan. Add the soy sauce and sesame oil. Add the stuffed squids and cook for 3 minutes.

Stir in any leftover stuffing mixture and adjust the seasoning. To serve, place 2 squid in each of 4 individual soup bowls, removing the cocktail sticks. Pour over the soup and garnish with chopped spring onion.

■ COOK'S TIP

The edible parts of a squid are the body and tentacles. The ink sac is sometimes used to colour and flavour a sauce.

■ COOK'S TIP

Make sure you use squid with bodies at least 15 cm/6 inches long for this recipe. Smaller specimens will burst during cooking and spoil the appearance of the finished *dish. The body cavity must be very well cleaned before being stuffed.*

9 FISH AND WATERCRESS SOUP

Preparation time:	YOU WILL NEED:
15 minutes	225 g/8 oz white fish fillets (see Cook's Tip)
Cooking time:	1 tablespoon cornflour
5-10 minutes	1 egg white, lightly beaten
	600 ml/1 pint Chinese stock (see recipe 2)
Serves 4	1 teaspoon finely chopped fresh root ginger
Calories:	1 bunch watercress, washed and trimmed
80 per portion	salt and pepper
	FOR THE GARNISH
	finely shredded spring onion
	sesame oil

Cut the fish into large slices. Dust them with the cornflour, then dip in the egg white to coat evenly.

Pour the stock into a medium saucepan. Add the ginger and bring the liquid to a rolling boil. Add the fish, a slice at a time. As soon as the slices float to the surface, add the watercress, salt and pepper. Reduce the heat and simmer for 1 minute.

Pour the soup into warmed serving bowls and scatter a little shredded spring onion over each one. Sprinkle with a few drops of sesame oil and serve immediately.

10 CHICKEN AND SWEETCORN SOUP

Preparation time:	YOU WILL NEED:
10 minutes	900 ml/1½ pints Chinese stock (see recipe 2), with a little of the cooked chicken reserved and chopped
Cooking time:	
20-25 minutes	350 g/12 oz sweetcorn kernels
	salt and pepper
Serves 4	2 teaspoons cornflour (optional)
	1 tablespoon water (optional)
Calories:	chopped spring onions, to garnish
120 per portion	(optional)

Pour the stock into a large saucepan and add 225 g/8 oz of the sweetcorn. Bring to the boil, add salt and pepper to taste, cover and simmer for 15 minutes. Liquidize until smooth, then return to the pan.

Reheat the soup. If it is not thick enough for your liking, blend the cornflour with the water and stir this thin paste into the soup and bring to the boil, stirring.

Add the remaining sweetcorn and the reserved chopped chicken. Simmer for 5 minutes. Adjust the seasoning before serving, garnished with spring onions if liked.

■ COOK'S TIP

Choose any firm white fish as the basis for this soup. Cod, haddock, monkfish or coley would be excellent; the flavour of sole and plaice is more delicate.

■ COOK'S TIP

This rich, filling soup is a good first course to precede a special fish dish such as Chinese steamed trout (recipe 67) or Steamed whole fish (recipe 55). As an alternative garnish, scatter very finely diced red pepper on top just before serving.

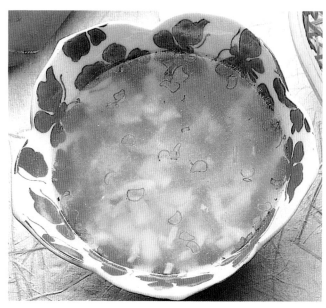

11 SPICY CHICKEN SOUP

Preparation time:
15-20 minutes

Cooking time:
15 minutes

Serves 4

Calories:
166 per portion

YOU WILL NEED:
3 tablespoons sunflower oil
½ large onion, thinly sliced
2 garlic cloves, crushed
1 teaspoon chopped fresh root ginger
½ teaspoon freshly ground black
  pepper
pinch of turmeric
175 g/6oz cooked chicken, coarsely
  chopped
1 tablespoon light soy sauce
1 litre/1¼ pints chicken stock
a handful of beanthread noodles,
  soaked till soft
75 g/3 oz bean sprouts
chopped spring onions, to garnish

Heat the oil in a medium saucepan and fry the onion, garlic and ginger until the onion is soft. Add the pepper, turmeric and chicken and stir for 30 seconds.

Add the soy sauce and stock and bring to the boil. Adjust the seasoning if necessary. Reduce the heat slightly and cook for 5 minutes.

Drain the noodles. Divide them equally among 4 warmed soup bowls. Divide the bean sprouts among the bowls and pour the soup on top. Serve hot, garnished with chopped spring onions.

12 CHICKEN AND HAM SOUP

Preparation time:
10-15 minutes

Cooking time:
5 minutes

Serves 4

Calories:
85 per portion

YOU WILL NEED:
100 g/4 oz chicken breast meat,
  skinned and boned
100 g/4 oz cooked ham
600 ml/1 pint Chinese stock (see
  recipe 2)
1 teaspoon finely chopped spring onion
salt

Slice the chicken and ham very thinly. Cut into small pieces.

Bring the stock to the boil in a medium saucepan. Add the pieces of chicken and ham and cook for 1 minute.

Place the spring onions and salt in a warmed soup tureen and pour the soup on top. Serve hot.

■ COOK'S TIP

Beanthread noodles, also called cellophane noodles, are made from mung bean flour. They must be soaked before cooking to make them soft.

■ COOK'S TIP

It is essential to use good, home-made stock for this simple but elegant soup. To save time, buy very finely sliced cooked ham from a delicatessen. You will find it easier to slice the chicken thinly if it is lightly frozen, but thaw it completely before use.

13 PORK, HAM AND BAMBOO SHOOT SOUP

Preparation time:
about 20 minutes

Cooking time:
10-15 minutes

Serves 4

Calories:
70 per portion

YOU WILL NEED:
50 g/2 oz pork fillet
2 teaspoons soy sauce
50 g/2 oz cooked ham
50 g/2 oz bamboo shoots
600 ml/1 pint Chinese stock (see recipe 2)
1 teaspoon salt
1 teaspoon rice wine or dry sherry

Slice the pork very thinly and toss it in the soy sauce. Shred the ham. Slice the bamboo shoots.

Bring the stock to the boil in a medium saucepan. Add the pork, reduce the heat slightly and cook for 5 minutes. Add the ham and bamboo shoots and bring back to the boil. Stir in the salt and sherry. Transfer the soup to 4 individual bowls and serve hot.

14 DUCK AND CABBAGE SOUP

Preparation time:
5 minutes

Cooking time:
about 1 hour 10 minutes

Serves 4-6

Calories:
431-288 per portion

YOU WILL NEED:
1 duck carcass, with giblets
1.2 litres/2 pints Chinese stock (see recipe 2) or water
2 slices fresh root ginger, peeled
450 g/1 lb Chinese cabbage, sliced
salt and pepper

Break up the duck carcass and place it in a large saucepan. Add the giblets and any other meat left over from the duck.

Cover with the stock or water, add the ginger, and bring to the boil. Skim, then lower the heat and simmer gently for at least 30 minutes.

Add the cabbage and salt and pepper to taste. Continue cooking for about 20 minutes.

Discard the pieces of duck carcass and the ginger slices. Taste and adjust the seasoning, if necessary. Pour into a warmed soup tureen and serve hot.

■ COOK'S TIP

Clear Chinese soups are characterized by a clarity and freshness that calls for top-quality ingredients, very briefly cooked. Because pork must be thoroughly cooked, *slice it as thinly as possible and test before serving.*

■ COOK'S TIP

Take care to skim off all the scum that rises to the surface in the first stage of cooking, so that the finished soup will be perfectly clear. Do not overcook the cabbage.

15 BEEF AND TOMATO SOUP

Preparation time:
about 20 minutes

Cooking time:
5 minutes

Serves 4

Calories:
250 per portion

YOU WILL NEED:
100 g/4 oz lean fillet steak
1 teaspoon cornflour
1½ teaspoons salt
225 g/8 oz tomatoes, peeled
(see Cook's Tip)
600 ml/1 pint Chinese stock (see recipe 2)
chopped spring onion, to garnish

Slice the steak very thinly and toss the strips in the cornflour, seasoned with a pinch of salt. Slice the tomatoes.

Place the stock in a medium saucepan and bring to a rolling boil. Add the steak, sliced tomatoes and remaining salt and bring back to the boil. Cook for 1 minute, stirring, and pour into 4 warmed serving bowls. Serve garnished with chopped spring onion.

16 SLICED PORK AND CABBAGE SOUP

Preparation time:
15 minutes, plus marinating

Cooking time:
5-10 minutes

Serves 4

Calories:
42 per portion

YOU WILL NEED:
100 g/4 oz pork fillet
1 tablespoon rice wine or dry sherry
1 tablespoon light soy sauce
100 g/4 oz Chinese cabbage
600 ml/1 pint Chinese stock (see recipe 2)
1 teaspoon salt

Slice the pork very thinly. Place the slices in a shallow glass or ceramic dish and pour over the rice wine or sherry and the soy sauce. Marinate for 10 minutes, turning the slices once or twice.

Cut the cabbage into 2.5 cm/1 inch lengths.

Place the stock in a medium saucepan and bring to the boil. Add the pork, stirring to keep the slices separate. Boil for 30 seconds, then add the cabbage and salt. Reduce the heat and simmer for 2 minutes. Transfer to individual serving bowls and serve hot.

■ COOK'S TIP

To skin tomatoes, score round the centre with a sharp pointed knife and immerse briefly in boiling water. Lift out with a slotted spoon and peel off the skins.

■ COOK'S TIP

This soup may be garnished, if liked, with freshly chopped herbs such as coriander or flat-leaf parsley, with shredded spring onion or watercress leaves. Add a

handful of pre-soaked beanthread (cellophane) noodles for a more substantial soup, and scatter freshly ground Szechuan pepper on top.

SNACKS & APPETIZERS

Chinese cuisine abounds in ideas for little savouries which can be served at any time of day. All make tempting starters, too. Those which can be eaten with the fingers are ideal party food. A tray of *dim-sum* – dumplings, wonton and dips – makes a delicious informal supper.

17 SESAME PRAWN TOASTS

Preparation time:
15 minutes

Cooking time:
5 minutes

Serves 6

Calories:
73 per portion

YOU WILL NEED:
25 g/1 oz pork fat, minced
125 g/5 oz peeled prawns, minced
1 egg white, lightly beaten
salt and pepper
3 teaspoons cornflour
2 thin slices crustless white bread
75 g/3 oz sesame seeds
sunflower oil for deep-frying

Mix together the pork fat, prawns, egg white, salt and pepper and cornflour. Spread this mixture on to the bread slices.

Place the sesame seeds on a flat plate, then press on the bread slices, prawn side down, until they are thickly coated with the seeds.

Heat the oil in a wok to 180 C/350 F or until a cube of day-old bread browns in 30 seconds. Carefully lower in the prawn toasts, spread side down, and deep-fry for 5 minutes, keeping them well-immersed. Lift out and drain on absorbent kitchen paper. Cut each slice into 4 fingers and serve hot.

18 STUFFED GREEN PEPPERS

Preparation time:
15 minutes

Cooking time:
30 minutes

Oven temperature:
200 C, 400 F, gas 6

Serves 4-6

Calories:
155-103 per portion

YOU WILL NEED:
1 tablespoon sunflower oil
1 garlic clove, crushed
1 piece fresh root ginger, peeled and
*   finely chopped*
225 g/8 oz lean minced pork
1 spring onion, chopped
1 celery stick, finely chopped
grated rind of 1 lemon
4 green peppers

Heat the oil in a wok or frying pan over a moderate heat. Add the garlic and stir-fry until lightly browned. Reduce the heat and add the ginger and pork. Stir-fry for 2 minutes. Add the spring onion, celery and lemon rind. Combine well and stir-fry for 30 seconds. Let the mixture cool slightly.

Cut the peppers into quarters and remove the core and seeds. Divide the mixture between the quarters, pressing it down well into the cavity.

Arrange the pepper quarters in an oiled ovenproof dish. Cook in a preheated oven for 25 minutes, until tender. Transfer to a warmed serving dish and serve immediately.

COOK'S TIP

Serve the toasts with drinks before dinner, with a platter of mixed crudites such as spring onions, celery sticks, radishes and baby carrots.

COOK'S TIP

These quartered peppers are easy to eat with the fingers and make a perfect dish for a party buffet. For an attractive platter, use a combination of green, red, orange and yellow peppers garnished with strips of contrasting colours.

19 RED OIL DUMPLINGS

Preparation time:
15-20 minutes

Cooking time:
about 20 minutes

Serves 4

Calories:
732 per portion

YOU WILL NEED:
450 g/1 lb plain flour, sifted
150 ml/¼ pint boiling water
85 ml/3 fl oz cold water
450 g/1 lb minced lean pork
100 g/4 oz peeled shrimps, minced
1 tablespoon freshly chopped
    root ginger
1 tablespoon freshly chopped
    spring onions
salt and pepper
1 tablespoon light soy sauce
1 teaspoon sugar
1 tablespoon water
2 leaves Chinese cabbage,
    finely chopped
2 teaspoons sesame oil
dipping sauce (see Cook's Tip)

Place the flour in a bowl, and stir in the boiling water to make a firm dough. Let stand for 2 minutes and add the cold water. Knead until smooth.

Combine the pork and shrimps with the remaining filling ingredients and beat well. Form the dough into a long sausage shape and cut into 5 cm/2 inch lengths. Roll each piece into a ball and flatten to make a pancake. Place 1 tablespoon of the filling on each pancake and fold it over to make a half-circle. Pinch the edges firmly together.

Cook the dumplings in batches in boiling water for about 5 minutes. Drain and keep hot. Serve with the dipping sauce.

20 WONTON

Preparation time:
25 minutes

Cooking time:
5 minutes

Serves 4-6

Calories:
800-560 per portion

YOU WILL NEED:
450 g/1 lb wonton skins
450 g/1 lb belly pork, minced
2 tablespoons light soy sauce
1 teaspoon brown sugar
1 teaspoon salt
350 g/12 oz frozen leaf spinach, thawed
sunflower oil for deep frying
soy sauce, to serve

Roll out the wonton skins and cut them into 5 cm/2 inch rounds. Put the pork, soy sauce, sugar and salt in a bowl and mix well. Squeeze the spinach in a clean cloth to extract as much liquid as possible, then add to the pork mixture and combine well.

Place a little of the pork and spinach mixture in the centre of each wonton paste round. Dampen the edges, twist around the filling and press together to seal.

Heat the oil to 180 C/350 F or until a cube of day-old bread browns in 30 seconds. Deep-fry the wonton in batches for about 5 minutes until golden. Drain on kitchen paper and serve hot with soy sauce.

▧ COOK'S TIP

For the sauce: mix together
2 tablespoons peanut butter,
2 teaspoons soy sauce,
1 teaspoon red chilli oil,
2 teaspoons chicken stock
and 1 crushed garlic clove.

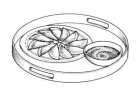

▧ COOK'S TIP

For best results when deep-frying, make sure the oil is hot enough before you start and do not put too many items in the oil at once, or the temperature will drop.

After removing each batch, make sure the oil comes back to the ideal temperature before proceeding.

21 FRIED WONTON WITH SWEET AND SOUR SAUCE

Preparation time: 20 minutes	**YOU WILL NEED:** 450 g/1 lb wonton skins
	3 tablespoons light soy sauce
Cooking time: about 20 minutes	1 tablespoon rice wine or dry sherry
	450 g/1 lb minced lean pork
	1 teaspoon brown sugar
Serves 4-6	1 garlic clove, crushed
	1 x 2.5 cm/1 inch piece fresh root
Calories:	ginger, peeled and finely chopped
650-450 per portion	225 g/8 oz frozen leaf spinach, thawed
(sauce 250 whole	sunflower oil for deep-frying
recipe)	FOR THE SAUCE
	(see Cook's Tip)

Cut out 5 cm/2 inch squares from the wonton skins. Put the soy sauce, sherry and pork in a bowl and mix well. Add the sugar, garlic and ginger. Squeeze excess liquid from the spinach in a clean cloth and add to the mixture. Combine well. Spoon 1 tablespoon of the mixture on to the centre of each wonton. Dampen the edges and fold to form triangles, pressing the edges together firmly so that the filling does not come out during frying.

Heat the oil to 180 C/350 F or until a cube of day-old bread browns in 30 seconds. Fry the wonton, a few at a time, for about 5 minutes until golden. Drain on kitchen paper and serve hot with sweet and sour sauce (see Cook's Tip).

22 COIN PURSE EGGS

Preparation time: 5 minutes	**YOU WILL NEED:** 6 tablespoons sunflower oil
	8 eggs
Cooking time: 15-20 minutes	salt and pepper
	3 tablespoons light soy sauce
	2 tablespoons white wine vinegar
Serves 4	4 tablespoons freshly chopped
	coriander or parsley
Calories:	
225 per portion	

Heat 2 tablespoons of the oil in a frying pan over a moderate heat. Break in 1 egg, if possible getting the yolk to one side. Add salt and pepper. Fry until the underside is set. Fold over one side of the white to cover the yolk completely. Increase the heat and cook until the underside is golden brown. Turn the egg over carefully and brown the other side. Transfer the egg to a warmed serving dish and keep warm. Cook the remaining eggs in the same way.

Mix together the soy sauce and wine vinegar and sprinkle over the eggs. Scatter the chopped herbs on top and serve while still warm.

▧ COOK'S TIP

For the sauce, stir-fry 2 crushed garlic cloves in 1 tablespoon sunflower oil. Add 2 tablespoons each light soy sauce, clear honey, wine vinegar and tomato purée.

Add 2 teaspoons each chilli sauce and Chinese wine, plus 2 teaspoons of a thin cornflour and water paste. Bring to the boil, cook 2 minutes.

▧ COOK'S TIP

In this Szechuan dish, the folded-over eggs are thought to look like purses containing golden coins – hence the charming name.

23 QUAIL'S EGGS ON TOAST WITH SHRIMPS

Preparation time:
10 minutes

Cooking time:
35 minutes

Serves 6

Calories:
379 per portion

YOU WILL NEED:
750 g/1½ lb peeled shrimps, mashed
50 g/2 oz pork fat, minced
1 teaspoon minced fresh root ginger
1 spring onion, finely chopped
1 egg white, lightly beaten
salt and pepper
½ teaspoon sesame oil
1 tablespoon Chinese wine
1½ teaspoons cornflour
2 sprigs parsley, finely chopped
1 slice cooked ham, finely chopped
8 slices crustless white bread, halved
16 quail's eggs, hard-boiled and shelled
sunflower oil for deep-frying

Combine the shrimps, fat, ginger, spring onion, egg white, salt and pepper, sesame oil, wine and cornflour. Beat until well blended. Mix together the parsley and ham.

Divide the shrimp mixture among the 16 slices of bread. Spread on in an even layer. Place a quail's egg firmly in the centre of each. Sprinkle on the ham and parsley and press into the filling.

Heat the oil in a wok to 180 C/350 F or until a cube of day-old bread browns in 30 seconds. Gently place the bread slices, filling side down, in the oil. Cook 2 or 3 at a time and fry until golden brown on both sides. Remove with a slotted spoon. Drain on kitchen paper and serve hot.

▨ COOK'S TIP

Serve this dish as an impressive starter to a special meal, as a component of mixed hors d'oeuvre or for a buffet. This recipe is from Canton, the southern province which is famed for the sophistication of its cuisine. Canned quail's eggs may be used if fresh eggs are unavailable.

24 BRAISED QUAIL'S EGGS

Preparation time:
about 25 minutes

Cooking time:
about 1 hour

Serves 4-6

Calories:
272-182 per portion

YOU WILL NEED:
24 quail's eggs
2 tablespoons light soy sauce
2 tablespoons cornflour
225 g/8 oz mangetout, trimmed
1-2 carrots, cut in thin strips
salt
1 teaspoon sugar
1 teaspoon sesame oil
300 ml/½ pint Chinese stock
sunflower oil for deep-frying
1 x 425 g/15 oz can straw mushrooms, drained

Put the quail's eggs in a bowl of cold water, place in a steamer and steam for 10 minutes. Remove the eggs and plunge them into cold water for 5 minutes. Shell the eggs, pour over the soy sauce and let marinate 20 minutes, turning frequently. Reserve the marinade and use 1 tablespoon cornflour to coat each egg. Mix the salt, sugar, sesame oil and remaining cornflour with the marinade to make a sauce.

Heat the oil in a pan until a cube of day-old bread browns in 30 seconds. Deep-fry the eggs until golden, drain and set aside. Pour off all but 2 tablespoons oil from the pan. Stir-fry the mangetout and carrots with a little sauce for 1½-2 minutes. Remove and arrange around the edge of a dish.

Heat 2 more tablespoons of oil in the pan. Stir-fry the mushrooms 30 seconds, add the eggs and remaining sauce and stir-fry until the sauce is smooth. Pour the eggs and mushrooms in the centre of the vegetables. Serve hot.

▨ COOK'S TIP

As a variation, or if mangetout are not available, substitute steamed asparagus spears, broccoli florets or small courgettes sliced very thinly lengthwise.

25 FRIED STEAMED DUMPLINGS

Preparation time:
20 minutes

Cooking time:
25 minutes

Serves 4-6

Calories:
630-440 per portion

YOU WILL NEED:
450 g/1 lb self-raising flour
pinch of salt
200-250 ml/7-8 fl oz water
sunflower oil for deep frying
FOR THE FILLING
350 g/12 oz minced pork
1 tablespoon light soy sauce
1 tablespoon Chinese wine or
     dry sherry
2 teaspoons sesame oil
2 spring onions, finely chopped
1 x 5 cm/2 inch piece fresh root ginger,
     peeled and finely chopped
100 g/4 oz canned bamboo shoots,
     drained and chopped

Sift the flour and salt into a bowl. Add enough water to mix to a firm dough. Divide in half and knead each piece, then form each one into a roll 5 cm/2 inches in diameter. Slice each roll into 14 pieces. Roll out to make 7.5 cm/3 inch circles.

Mix all the filling ingredients together and divide between the rounds, placing it in the centre. Gather up the sides of the dough around the filling to meet at the top, then firmly twist to seal tightly. Arrange the dumplings in a steamer lined with a piece of moist muslin and steam for 20 minutes. Drain.

Heat the oil in a wok or pan until a cube of day-old bread browns in 30 seconds. Fry the dumplings in small batches for 5-6 minutes until golden. Drain on absorbent kitchen paper and serve at once.

26 STEAMED MEAT DUMPLINGS

Preparation time:
30 minutes, plus
rising

Cooking time:
20 minutes

Serves 4

Calories:
828 per portion

YOU WILL NEED:
500 g/1¼ lb plain flour
4 teaspoons baking powder
250 ml/8 fl oz water
450 g/1 lb minced pork, fat and lean
1 tablespoon Chinese wine or
     dry sherry
3 tablespoons light soy sauce
2 teaspoons sugar
salt
1 tablespoon sesame oil
2 teaspoons finely chopped fresh
     ginger root
1 teaspoon cornflour

Sift the flour and baking powder together into a bowl. Add the water and knead well. Cover with a damp cloth and place a small plate on top. Leave to rise for 2 hours.

Combine the pork with the wine or sherry, soy sauce, sugar, salt, sesame oil, ginger and cornflour.

Divide the dough in half. Knead lightly and roll each half into a sausage shape 5 cm/2 inches in diameter. Slice each into about 15 rounds. Flatten the rounds then roll out to make circles 7.5 cm/3 inches in diameter.

Place a tablespoon of filling on each circle. Gather up the sides of the dough to meet at the top, and twist to seal tightly. Arrange the dumplings 1 cm/½ inch apart on a piece of damp muslin in a steamer. Cover and steam vigorously for 20 minutes. Drain if necessary and serve hot.

▨ COOK'S TIP

This recipe is a good example of 'cross-cooking', in which the dumplings are first steamed to cook them and then deep-fried to give them a delicious crispy finish.

▨ COOK'S TIP

Any left-over dumplings can be reheated successfully either by steaming vigorously for 5 minutes or by shallow-frying in a little hot oil for 6-7 minutes, turning them over once during cooking. Serve with Sweet and sour sauce (see Cook's Tip recipe 21).

27 CRISPY SPRING ROLLS

Preparation time:
20-25 minutes

Cooking time:
15-20 minutes

Serves 4-6

Calories:
400-267 per portion

YOU WILL NEED:
225 g/8 oz plain flour
pinch of salt
1 egg
sunflower oil for deep-frying
FOR THE FILLING
1 tablespoon sunflower oil
225 g/8 oz lean pork, shredded
1 garlic clove, crushed
2 celery sticks, sliced
100 g/4 oz mushrooms, sliced
2 spring onions, chopped
100 g/4 oz bean sprouts
100 g/4 oz peeled prawns
2 tablespoons light soy sauce

Sift the flour and salt into a bowl. Add the egg and about 300 ml/½ pint cold water to make a smooth batter. Lightly oil a 20 cm/8 inch frying pan and set over a moderate heat. Pour in enough batter to cover the base of the pan. Cook until the underside is pale golden, turn and cook the other side. Repeat until all the batter is used.

To make the filling, heat the oil, add the pork and brown quickly. Add the garlic and vegetables and stir-fry 2 minutes. Mix in the prawns and soy sauce. Allow to cool.

Place 2-3 tablespoons of the filling in the centre of each pancake. Fold in the sides and form a tight roll, sealing the edge with a little flour and water paste. Deep-fry in hot oil until golden, cooking 2 rolls at a time. Drain and serve hot.

▨COOK'S TIP

Many Chinese and other South-East Asian recipes use fish and meat together, and many meat dishes include fish sauces or pastes as a flavouring agent.

The result is a distinctively savoury blend of flavours at its best when offset, as here, with a combination of fresh vegetables.

28 STEAMED SCALLOPS IN BLACK BEAN SAUCE

Preparation time:
5 minutes

Cooking time:
8 minutes

Serves 4

Calories:
168 per portion

YOU WILL NEED:
12 scallops in their shells
2 tablespoons sunflower oil
2 tablespoons salted black beans,
*   soaked, drained and crushed*
1 fresh chilli, seeded and finely chopped
1 garlic clove, crushed
2 spring onions, finely chopped
2 tablespoons soy sauce
2 teaspoons sugar
3 tablespoons Chinese stock
*   (see recipe 2)*
2 teaspoons cornflour

Clean the scallops (see Cook's Tip) and replace them on their shells with the corals. Place in a bamboo steamer set over a saucepan or wok of boiling water and steam gently for 5-6 minutes.

Heat the oil in a wok and add the black beans, chilli, garlic and spring onions. Stir-fry for 1 minute and add the soy sauce and sugar.

Blend the stock with the cornflour and add it to the sauce. Cook, stirring continuously, until the sauce has thickened.

Arrange the scallops on a serving dish and pour the hot sauce over. Serve immediately.

▨COOK'S TIP

Open the shells by inserting a knife and twisting it. Discard the fringe surrounding the white flesh. Separate the coral and set aside. Ease the scallop from the shell.

29 PRAWN AND BEANSPROUT FRITTERS

Preparation time: 20 minutes	**YOU WILL NEED:** 100 g/4 oz peeled prawns, minced
	225 g/8 oz beansprouts
Cooking time: 6-8 minutes	4 shallots, thinly sliced
	½ small onion, finely sliced
	2 garlic cloves, crushed
Serves 6-8	2 tablespoons freshly chopped coriander leaves (optional)
Calories: 180-140 per portion	2 teaspoons freshly grated root ginger
	2 tablespoons grated coconut flesh (optional)
	50 g/2 oz rice flour or self-raising flour
	1 teaspoon baking powder
	1 teaspoon ground coriander
	½ teaspoon chilli powder
	3 tablespoons water
	1 egg, beaten,
	salt and pepper
	sunflower oil for deep-frying
	lemon slices, to garnish

Place all the ingredients, except the oil and lemon slices, in a bowl. Combine well. Form the mixture into small balls about the size of walnuts, or flatten them like fish-cakes.

Heat the oil to 180 C/350 F or until a cube of day-old bread browns in 30 seconds. Fry the fritters for 1½-2 minutes until golden. Remove with a slotted spoon and drain on absorbent kitchen paper. Transfer to a serving dish and garnish with lemon slices. Serve hot or cold.

▓ COOK'S TIP

These tiny fritters are ideal to serve with pre-dinner drinks. Try using crabmeat or flaked smoked fish instead of the prawns, or if you prefer, omit the fish and increase the proportion of beansprouts for a delicious vegetarian snack.

30 CRAB AND WATER CHESTNUT FRITTERS

Preparation time: about 30 minutes, plus standing	**YOU WILL NEED:** 350 g/12 oz crab meat, finely chopped
	50 g/2 oz pork fat, minced
	4 water chestnuts, peeled and finely chopped
Cooking time: 10-15 minutes	1 egg white
	2 tablespoons cornflour
Serves 4	salt and pepper
	1 tablespoon Chinese wine or dry sherry
Calories: 262 per portion	sunflower oil for deep-frying

Place the crab meat in a bowl with the pork fat and water chestnuts and blend well. Add the egg white, cornflour, salt and pepper and wine or sherry and mix together.

Heat the oil in a wok or pan to 180 C/350 F or until a cube of day-old bread browns in 30 seconds. Using a teaspoon, scoop up 1 spoonful of the crab mixture at a time and lower it into the hot oil. Fry the balls until they are golden brown, remove with a slotted spoon and drain on absorbent kitchen paper. They should be crisp on the outside and tender inside. Serve hot.

▓ COOK'S TIP

Crispy fish fritters make a delicious meal. Experiment with different fillings, substituting prawns for the crabmeat or any firm white fish like cod or haddock.

31 JELLIED CHICKEN

Preparation time:
25-30 minutes, plus
setting

Cooking time:
1¾ hours

Serves 4

Calories:
637 per portion

YOU WILL NEED:
1.5 kg/3-3½ lb roasting chicken
2 litres/3½ pints water
3 spring onions
3 slices fresh root ginger
salt
2 tablespoons Chinese wine or
  dry sherry
cucumber slices, to garnish

Place the chicken in a saucepan, cover with the water and bring to the boil. Reduce the heat slightly and cook for about 1 hour. Remove the chicken, reserving the cooking liquid. Take the meat off the bone, separating the skin, and place in a pudding basin.

Cover the meat with the cooking liquid. Add the chicken skin, spring onions, ginger, salt and wine or sherry. Place the basin in a steamer or double saucepan and steam vigorously for at least 45 minutes. Discard the skin, spring onions and ginger.

When the basin is cool, place it in the refrigerator for 6-8 hours or until the juice has set to a jelly. To serve, turn out on to a flat plate and garnish with cucumber slices.

32 SZECHUAN BANG-BANG CHICKEN

Preparation time:
15-20 minutes

Cooking time:
15 minutes

Serves 4

Calories:
92 per portion

YOU WILL NEED:
175 g/6 oz boned and skinned
  chicken breast
1 lettuce heart
FOR THE SAUCE
1 tablespoon tahini (sesame paste)
1 tablespoon light soy sauce
2 teaspoons vinegar
1 teaspoon chilli sauce
1 teaspoon sugar
2 tablespoons Chinese stock
  (see recipe 2)

Place the chicken meat in a saucepan and cover with cold water. Bring to the boil, then reduce the heat and simmer gently for 10 minutes. Drain and beat the meat with a rolling pin until it is soft. Leave to cool slightly.

Cut the lettuce leaves into shreds and place them on a serving dish. Pull the chicken meat into shreds with your fingers and arrange on top of the lettuce.

Mix together all the ingredients for the sauce and pour evenly over the chicken just before serving.

▦COOK'S TIP

Use the chicken bones with any leftover liquid as the basis for a stock, adding onion and celery, or incorporating them in a classic Chinese stock (see recipe 2).

▦COOK'S TIP

The unusual name of this dish refers to the fact that the chicken is beaten with a rolling pin to soften it. If you cannot obtain tahini (sesame paste), an acceptable
substitute is peanut butter creamed with a little sesame oil.

33 CHICKEN SPRING ROLLS

Preparation time:
30 minutes

Cooking time:
about 10 minutes

Makes 20

Calories:
120 per roll

YOU WILL NEED:
50 g/2 oz cellophane noodles, soaked
    in water for 10 minutes and cut
    into 2.5 cm/1 inch pieces
450 g/1 lb chicken breast meat,
    cut into thin strips
2 tablespoons dried wood ears, soaked
    in warm water for 20 minutes
    and finely chopped
3 garlic cloves, finely chopped
3 shallots, finely chopped
225 g/8 oz crabmeat
pepper
sunflower oil for deep-frying
spring onion tassels, to garnish
    (see Cook's Tip)
FOR THE WRAPPERS
4 eggs, beaten
20 dried rice papers

For the filling, put the ingredients in a bowl and mix well. Divide into 20 portions and shape into small cylinder shapes.

Brush beaten egg over the entire surface of each piece of rice paper. Leave for a few minutes until soft. Place the filling along the curved edge of the paper, roll once, then fold over the sides to enclose and continue rolling.

Heat the oil until a cube of day-old bread browns in 30 seconds. Fry the spring rolls, 5 or 6 at a time, until golden all over. Drain well on absorbent kitchen paper. Serve hot or warm, garnished with spring onion tassels.

▨COOK'S TIP

Spring onion tassels: cut the onions to 7.5 cm/3 inches long. Cut lengthwise through the stalk several times to within 4 cm/1½ inches of the end. Place in iced water for 1 hour.

34 FIVE-SPICE PORK SPARERIBS

Preparation time:
20 minutes, plus
marinating

Cooking time:
20 or 45 minutes
(see recipe)

Oven temperature:
200 C, 400 F, gas 6

Serves 8

Calories:
278 per portion

YOU WILL NEED:
1 kg/2-¼ lb pork spareribs
FOR THE MARINADE
1 teaspoon salt
2 tablespoons sugar
2 tablespoons brandy, whisky, rum
    or vodka
2 tablespoons light soy sauce
2 tablespoons hoisin sauce
1 tablespoon dark soy sauce
1 teaspoon five-spice powder
1 teaspoon curry powder (optional)

Cut the pork into individual ribs if this has not already been done by the butcher. Place them in a bowl, add the remaining ingredients and blend together. Leave to marinate for 1 hour, turning them over once or twice.

Cook the ribs in the marinade in a preheated oven for 40-45 minutes, turning them once halfway during cooking. Alternatively remove the ribs from the marinade and grill under a preheated grill for 15-20 minutes, turning them every 5 minutes or so until browned all over.

Chop each rib into 2-3 bite-sized pieces if you have a meat cleaver. Otherwise serve them whole with the sauce poured over them. If you have grilled the ribs, make a sauce by bringing the marinade to the boil in a saucepan with a little stock or water.

▨COOK'S TIP

This versatile dish can be cooked in the oven, under a grill, or outside on a barbecue. If cooking on a barbecue, slightly less time is required, but the ribs will need to be turned over more frequently to make sure they are evenly browned.

35 DEEP-FRIED PRAWN BALLS

Preparation time:	YOU WILL NEED:
15 minutes, plus standing	450 g/1 lb peeled prawns, finely chopped
	50 g/2 oz pork fat, finely chopped
Cooking time:	1 egg white
20 minutes	2 tablespoons cornflour
	1 tablespoons brandy or rum
Serves 4	1 teaspoon finely chopped fresh root ginger
Calories:	salt and pepper
320 per portion	sunflower oil for deep-frying
	celery leaves, to garnish

Mix the prawns with the pork fat in a bowl. Add the egg white, cornflour, brandy or rum, ginger and salt and pepper to taste. Stir well and leave to stand for 30 minutes.

Divide the mixture into 24 equal portions and form into small balls. Heat the oil to 180 C/350 F or until a cube of day-old bread browns in 30 seconds. Deep-fry the balls in batches until golden. Drain on absorbent kitchen paper.

Just before serving, reheat the oil and re-fry the balls for a few seconds. Drain again and place in a serving bowl. Garnish with celery leaves and serve immediately.

36 SAVOURY DUMPLINGS

Preparation time:	YOU WILL NEED:
1½-2 hours	450 g/1 lb plain flour
	300 ml/½ pint water
Cooking time:	450 g/1 lb pork
about 20 minutes	225 g/8 oz bamboo shoots
	3-4 spring onions, finely chopped
Makes 30-35	3 slices fresh root ginger, peeled and finely chopped
Calories:	salt
80-69 per dumpling	2 teaspoons sugar
	2 teaspoons light soy sauce
	2 tablespoons Chinese wine
	2 tablespoons Chinese stock (see recipe 2)
	1 teaspoon sesame oil
	1 small cabbage, separated into leaves
	dipping sauce (see Cook's Tip)

Sift the flour into a mixing bowl, pour in the water and mix to a stiff dough. Knead for 5 minutes, then cover the bowl with a clean damp cloth and allow to stand for 10 minutes.

To make the dumpling filling, coarsely chop the meat and bamboo shoots and place in a bowl. Add the spring onions, ginger, salt, sugar, soy sauce, wine, stock and sesame oil. Blend thoroughly.

Divide the dough in half and form each piece into a sausage shape. Cut each roll into 16-18 slices. Flatten the rounds, then roll into circles about 7.5 cm/3 inches in diameter. Fill the dumplings (see Cook's Tip).

Line a steamer with cabbage leaves. Put on the dumplings, cover and steam for 20 minutes. Serve hot with the dip.

COOK'S TIP

These savouries can be prepared up to 3 hours in advance. Reheat in a moderate oven (180°C, 350°F, gas 4) for 10-15 minutes before serving.

COOK'S TIP

To fill the dumplings, place 1 tablespoon of filling at the centre of each circle of dough. Gather up the edges of dough and twist together at the top to seal tightly. For *a dipping sauce, mix 2 tablespoons of soy sauce with one tablespoon of vinegar.*

FISH

The long coastline of China, its swift rivers and enormous lakes, have ensured that Chinese cuisine is a rich source of imaginative recipes for fish and seafood. Try some new ideas for familiar fish – Trout with salted cabbage, Soy-braised cod steaks, Sole with satay sauce, Szechuan prawns with chilli and tomato – as well as the less well-known but equally delicious Red mullet in black bean sauce or Sweet and sour carp.

37 POACHED PRAWNS WITH PIQUANT DIP SAUCE

Preparation time:
10 minutes

Cooking time:
1-2 minutes

Serves 4

Calories:
180 per portion

YOU WILL NEED:
450 g/1 lb uncooked prawns
1 teaspoon salt
4-5 slices fresh root ginger, unpeeled
FOR THE DIP SAUCE
2 tablespoons sunflower oil
2-3 slices fresh root ginger, peeled
    and shredded
2-3 spring onions, shredded
2-3 fresh green and red chillies, seeded
    and finely shredded
3 tablespoons light soy sauce
1 tablespoon wine vinegar
1 tablespoon sake or dry sherry
pinch of sugar
1 teaspoon sesame oil

Wash the prawns. Trim off the heads, whiskers and legs but leave the tails attached to make them easier to hold.

Bring 2 litres/3½ pints water to the boil in a large pan with the salt and sliced ginger. Add the prawns and poach for 1-2 minutes only, until they have changed colour. Drain well.

To make the dip sauce, heat the oil in a small pan until it is very hot. Place the shredded ginger, spring onions and fresh chillies in a bowl. Slowly pour the hot oil over and stir in the remaining ingredients. Serve with the prawns.

38 CRAB OMELETTE

Preparation time:
10 minutes

Cooking time:
1-2 minutes

Serves 3-4

Calories:
360-270 per portion

YOU WILL NEED:
2 spring onions
4 eggs, beaten
salt
3 tablespoons sunflower oil
2 slices fresh root ginger, peeled
    and shredded
175 g/6 oz crab meat
1 tablespoon sake or dry sherry
1 tablespoon light soy sauce
2 teaspoons sugar
FOR THE GARNISH
½ lettuce, shredded
1 tomato
seedless grapes

Cut the white part of the spring onions into 2.5 cm/1 inch lengths. Chop the green part finely. Beat the eggs lightly in a bowl and add the chopped onion stalks with salt to taste.

Heat the oil in a frying pan and add the white parts of the onions with the ginger, the crab and sake or sherry. Stir-fry for a few seconds, then add the soy sauce and sugar.

Reduce the heat, pour in the egg mixture and cook for a further 30 seconds. Transfer to a warmed serving plate and scatter shredded lettuce around the edge. Make a tomato 'water-lily' (see Cook's Tip). Place one half of the tomato in the centre of the omelette with a grape in the middle.

▓ COOK'S TIP

There is no perceptible difference in flavour between green and red chillies. Generally, the smaller the chilli the hotter it will be. When working with chillies, *take care not to touch your eyes or lips, and always wash your hands immediately afterwards.*

▓ COOK'S TIP

To make a tomato waterlily, with a small sharp knife make small, even zigzag cuts around the middle of a firm tomato and carefully separate the two halves.

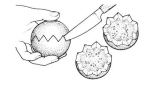

39 PAPER-WRAPPED FISH

Preparation time:
15 minutes

Cooking time:
3 minutes

Serves 4

Calories:
300 per portion

YOU WILL NEED:
4 x 100 g/4 oz fillets of sole or plaice
pinch of salt
2 tablespoons Chinese wine or
    dry sherry
1 tablespoon vegetable oil
2 tablespoons shredded spring onion
2 tablespoons shredded fresh
    root ginger
vegetable oil for deep frying
spring onion tassels, to garnish
    (see recipe 33)

Cut the fish fillets into 2.5 cm/1 inch squares. Sprinkle with the salt and toss in the wine or sherry.

Cut out 15 cm/6 inch squares of greaseproof paper and brush them with the oil. Place a piece of fish on each square of paper and arrange some shredded spring onion and ginger on top. Fold the pieces of paper into envelopes (see Cook's Tip), tucking in the flaps to secure them.

Heat the oil in a wok or deep saucepan to 180 C/350 F or until a cube of day-old bread browns in 30 seconds. Deep-fry the wrapped fish for 3 minutes. Drain and arrange on a warmed serving dish. Garnish with spring onion tassels and serve at once. Each person unwraps his own parcels with chopsticks.

40 SHREDDED FISH WITH CELERY

Preparation time:
20-25 minutes

Cooking time:
4 minutes

Serves 4

Calories:
111 per portion

YOU WILL NEED:
225 g/8 oz cod or haddock fillet
1 teaspoon salt
1 tablespoon Chinese wine or
    dry sherry
1 egg white
1 tablespoon cornflour
1 celery heart
sunflower oil for deep-frying
FOR THE GARNISH
25 g/1 oz cooked ham, thinly shredded
celery leaves

Remove the skin from the fish and cut the flesh into thin shreds. Place in a bowl and sprinkle with a pinch of salt. Add the wine or sherry, the egg white and then the cornflour. Leave the fish to stand, turning it over once or twice.

Cut the celery heart into thin shreds. Heat 2 tablespoons of oil in a wok and stir-fry the celery with the remaining salt for about 1½ minutes. Transfer to a warmed serving dish.

Heat the remaining oil in the wok or a deep pan over a moderate heat. Deep-fry the shredded fish for about 2 minutes, separating them with a pair of chopsticks. When all the shreds are floating on the surface of the oil, scoop them out with a slotted spoon, drain on absorbent kitchen paper and arrange in the middle of the celery. Strew the cooked ham on top and garnish with celery leaves.

Serve this dish hot or cold.

■ COOK'S TIP

To make an envelope, place the paper diagonally and put the filling in the nearest triangle. Fold the corners in the sequence shown and tuck the last corner in securely.

■ COOK'S TIP

As an variation on celery, try shredded celeriac. This root vegetable has the fine flavour of celery but looks more like a rough-skinned swede. It can be stir-fried as here or served raw, grated and sprinkled with salt and lemon juice .

41 CANTONESE CRAB IN BLACK BEAN SAUCE

Preparation time:
20-25 minutes, plus marinating

Cooking time:
about 10 minutes

Serves 4

Calories:
195 per portion

YOU WILL NEED:
2 × 450-500 g/1-1¼ lb crabs
1 tablespoon light soy sauce
2 tablespoons Chinese wine or
  dry sherry
1 tablespoon cornflour
2 tablespoons black bean sauce
3 tablespoons corn oil
1 garlic clove, crushed and finely
  chopped
4 slices fresh root ginger, peeled
  and finely chopped
2-3 spring onions, finely chopped
1 tablespoon white wine vinegar
2-3 tablespoons Chinese stock
  (see recipe 2) or water

Wash the crab shells and separate the legs and claws. Crack the claws with the back of a cleaver. Crack the shells into 2-3 pieces. Discard the feathery gills and the sac.

Place the crab pieces in a bowl and add the soy sauce, wine or sherry and cornflour. Marinate 10 minutes. Place the black bean sauce in a small bowl and mash with a spoon.

Heat the oil in a preheated wok or frying pan. Add the garlic, ginger and spring onions to flavour the oil, then add the crushed black bean sauce, stirring until smooth. Put in the crab pieces, stirring constantly for 1½-2 minutes. Add the vinegar and stock or water. Continue cooking, still stirring, until the sauce is thickened. Serve hot.

42 BRAISED PRAWNS

Preparation time:
5 minutes, plus marinating

Cooking time:
about 5 minutes

Serves 4

Calories:
180 per portion

YOU WILL NEED:
1 teaspoon salt
1 egg white
2 tablespoons cornflour
225 g/8 oz raw prawns, peeled
225 g/8 oz lard
2 tablespoons Chinese wine or
  dry sherry
4 tablespoons Chinese stock (see
  recipe 2)
1 tablespoon water
1 teaspoon sesame oil
shredded lettuce, to garnish

Mix the salt with the egg white and 1 tablespoon of the cornflour. Add the prawns and leave to marinate in the refrigerator for 1-2 hours.

Heat the lard in a pan. Add the prawns and stir to separate them, then lift out with a slotted spoon. Pour off the excess fat, leaving a small amount in the pan. Add the wine or sherry, stock and prawns and bring to the boil. Combine the remaining cornflour with the water to make a paste. Add to the pan and continue to cook, stirring, until the sauce is thickened. Add the sesame oil. Transfer to a platter and serve immediately, garnished with shredded lettuce.

▧ COOK'S TIP

This classic Cantonese dish is best eaten with the fingers. Provide your guests with finger bowls of warm water and plenty of paper napkins.

▧ COOK'S TIP

The shells of prawns come away very easily if you first straighten out the body, then press the head and tail together and pull them apart again. This loosens the shell and makes it possible to remove it in one piece.

43 PRAWNS WITH ALMONDS

Preparation time:
4 minutes

Cooking time:
7 minutes

Serves 4

Calories:
300 per portion

YOU WILL NEED:
2 tablespoons sunflower oil
75 g/3 oz blanched almonds
350 g/12 oz peeled prawns
2 teaspoons cornflour
1 heaped teaspoon finely chopped fresh
    root ginger
1 small garlic clove, crushed
1 celery stick, finely chopped
2 teaspoons light soy sauce
2 teaspoons Chinese wine or dry sherry
2 tablespoons water
pepper
spring onion tassels, to garnish
    (see recipe 33)

Brush a frying pan with a little of the oil and add the almonds.
Place the pan over a moderate heat and toss the almonds until
golden. Drain on absorbent kitchen paper.

Place the prawns in a bowl with the cornflour, ginger and
garlic and mix well.

Heat the remaining oil in the pan. Add the prawn mixture
and celery and stir-fry for 2-3 minutes. Add the soy sauce,
wine or sherry, water and pepper to taste. Bring to the boil,
add the almonds and heat for 30 seconds. Serve hot, garnished
with spring onion tassels.

44 GINGER AND SPRING ONION CRAB

Preparation time:
25-30 minutes, plus
marinating

Cooking time:
about 6 minutes

Serves 4

Calories:
207 per portion

YOU WILL NEED:
1 x 750 g/1¼ lb crab
2 tablespoons Chinese wine or
    dry sherry
1 tablespoon Chinese stock (see
    recipe 2) or water
2 tablespoons cornflour
4 slices fresh ginger root, peeled
    and finely chopped
4 spring onions, finely chopped
3 tablespoons sunflower oil
1 teaspoon salt
1 tablespoon light soy sauce
2 teaspoons sugar

Wash the crab shells and separate the legs and claws. Crack
the claws with the back of a cleaver. Crack the shells into
2-3 pieces. Discard the feathery gills and the sac.

Place the crab in a bowl with 1 tablespoon of the wine or
sherry, the stock or water and the cornflour. Stir once or twice
and leave to marinate for 10 minutes.

Combine the chopped ginger and spring onion. In a wok or
frying pan heat the oil until it is hot, then add the crab pieces
and stir-fry for 1 minute. Add the ginger and onion, the salt,
soy sauce, sugar and remaining wine or sherry. Cook for
about 5 minutes, stirring constantly. Add a little water if the
mixture becomes very dry.

Serve hot.

▧ COOK'S TIP

*To blanch almonds, drop
them into boiling water,
bring back to the boil and
drain. Squeeze the nuts while
warm to slip them out of
their skins. Blot dry.*

▧ COOK'S TIP

*When a dish like this, which
must be eaten with the
fingers, is on the menu, it is
a good idea to choose other
dishes which are relatively
easy to eat. Choose a light*
*soup as the first course, and a
main course such as Diced
turkey with celery (recipe
105) in which the meat is
already prepared in bite-sized
pieces.*

45   SWEET AND SOUR FISH

Preparation time:
5 minutes

Cooking time:
7 minutes

Serves 4

Calories:
180 per portion

YOU WILL NEED:
¼ teaspoon ground ginger
2 teaspoons cornflour
450 g/1 lb haddock or cod fillets,
    cut into small pieces
1 tablespoon corn oil
freshly chopped parsley, to garnish
FOR THE SAUCE
1 x 227 g/8 oz can tomatoes, drained
    and chopped
1 tablespoon light soy sauce
1 tablespoon tomato purée
2 teaspoons cornflour
5 tablespoons water
2 tablespoons Chinese wine or
    dry sherry
1 teaspoon brown sugar

Mix the ginger with the cornflour and use to coat the fish. Heat the oil in a wok or frying pan, add the fish and stir-fry for 2-3 minutes. Remove from the pan with a slotted spoon and keep warm.

Wipe the wok clean with absorbent kitchen paper and reduce the heat. Place the tomatoes and soy sauce in the wok. Mix the remaining sauce ingredients together, then pour this mixture into the wok and cook, stirring, until thickened. Add the fish and heat through for a few seconds. Transfer to a warmed serving dish, sprinkle the parsley on top and serve at once.

▨ COOK'S TIP

To make this sauce even richer and thicker, try sun-dried tomatoes instead of tomato purée. Chop them finely before adding to the pan, use a little of the oil in which they are preserved for a smooth texture.

46   FISH SLICES WITH WINE SAUCE

Preparation time:
10-15 minutes

Cooking time:
7 minutes

Serves 4

Calories:
283 per portion

YOU WILL NEED:
450 g/1 lb plaice or sole fillets
1 egg white, lightly beaten
2 tablespoons cornflour
5 tablespoons water
vegetable oil for deep-frying (see
    Cook's Tip)
1½ teaspoons salt
1 teaspoon sugar
300 ml/ ½ pint Chinese stock (see recipe 2)
4 tablespoons Chinese wine or
    dry sherry
1 teaspoon sesame oil, to garnish

Cut the fish fillets into large pieces, leaving the skin on. Coat them with egg white. Combine the cornflour with the water to make a thin paste and pour over the fish, turning the pieces.

Heat the oil in a wok or deep pan. Before it becomes too hot, add the fish pieces one by one, reserving the leftover cornflour mixture, and fry over a moderate heat for 1 minute. Use chopsticks to keep the slices separate. Scoop the fish out with a slotted spoon and drain on absorbent kitchen paper.

Pour off the oil, and return the fish to the pan with the salt, sugar, stock and wine or sherry. Bring to the boil, reduce the heat and simmer for 2 minutes. Increase the heat and slowly pour the remaining cornflour mixture into the wok, tilting it to cover all the fish. As soon as the sauce has thickened, sprinkle over the sesame oil and serve.

▨ COOK'S TIP

Sunflower oil is a good all-round vegetable oil for frying, but other suitable oils include groundnut (arachide) oil, grapeseed oil and corn oil.

47 FISH SLICES IN CHILLI SAUCE

Preparation time:
about 15 minutes

Cooking time:
6 minutes

Serves 4

Calories:
170 per portion

YOU WILL NEED:
450 g/1 lb cod or plaice fillets
1 tablespoon plain flour
300 ml/ ½ pint sunflower oil
FOR THE SAUCE
½ tablespoon finely chopped fresh
   root ginger
1 tablespoon finely chopped
   spring onion
3 tablespoons sherry
1 tablespoon light soy sauce
2 teaspoons sugar
1 teaspoon salt
1 teaspoon white wine vinegar
1-2 tablespoons chilli purée

Cut the fish fillets into 5 cm/2 inch slices and coat them with the flour.

Heat the oil in a wok or frying pan over a moderate heat. Add the fish slices and cook for 3 minutes, separating them with a pair of chopsticks. Lift the fish from the oil with a slotted spoon. Let the oil become hot again and return the fish slices to the pan for a few seconds to crisp. Remove from the pan and drain well on absorbent kitchen paper.

Pour off most of the oil from the pan, leaving about 1 tablespoon. Combine the ingredients for the sauce and add to the pan. Stir-fry for 30 seconds. Add the fish slices and stir-fry for 1 minute. Serve immediately.

▨ COOK'S TIP

Tastes vary as to the degree of hotness which can be tolerated in spicy sauces such as this. If you use chilli sauce instead of chill purée, remember that it is very

much hotter and half the quantity given here will be enough for most palates.

48 SZECHUAN PRAWNS IN CHILLI AND TOMATO SAUCE

Preparation time:
20-25 minutes

Cooking time:
5 minutes

Serves 4

Calories:
106 per portion

YOU WILL NEED:
225 g/8 oz raw prawns, peeled
1 egg white
2 teaspoons cornflour
sunflower oil for deep-frying
1 spring onion, finely chopped
2 slices fresh root ginger, peeled
   and finely chopped
1 garlic clove, finely chopped
1 tablespoon Chinese wine or
   dry sherry
1 tablespoon tomato purée
1 tablespoon chilli sauce
lettuce leaves
tomato rose (see Cook's Tip)

Mix a pinch of the salt with the prawns, add the egg white and dust with cornflour.

Heat the oil in a wok or deep pan. Add the prawns, stirring to keep them separate, and deep-fry for 30 seconds over moderate heat. Remove from the wok and drain.

Pour off all but 1 tablespoon of oil from the wok. Over a high heat, stir-fry the spring onion, ginger and garlic for a few seconds. Add the prawns and stir-fry for 1 minute. Add the wine, tomato purée and chilli sauce, stirring until the sauce is well blended. Line a dish with lettuce and pour the prawns and sauce into the centre. Serve immediately, garnished with a tomato rose.

▨ COOK'S TIP

For a tomato rose, remove the skin in one strip about 1 cm/ ½ inch wide. With the flesh side inside, curl it from the base end, forming a flower shape.

49 RED MULLET IN BLACK BEAN SAUCE

Preparation time:
15 minutes

Cooking time:
15-20 minutes

Serves 4

Calories:
332 per portion

YOU WILL NEED:

1 x 450 g/1 lb red mullet

1 teaspoon salt

1 tablespoon cornflour

2 tablespoons salted black beans

4 tablespoons sunflower oil

1 garlic clove, crushed

2 slices fresh root ginger, peeled
    and thinly shredded

1 small green pepper, corned, seeded
    and sliced

2 tablespoons Chinese wine or
    dry sherry

Scale and clean the fish. Slash both sides diagonally as far as the bone at intervals of 2 cm/¾ inch. Dry thoroughly, then rub the fish with the salt inside and out. Coat with cornflour.

Place the black beans in a small bowl and crush with the back of a spoon.

Heat 2 tablespoons oil in a wok or frying pan and stir-fry the garlic, ginger and green pepper. Add the crushed black beans and blend well. Remove this mixture from the wok with a slotted spoon.

Heat the remaining oil in the wok and fry the fish for 4-6 minutes, turning it once. Return the green pepper and black bean mixture to the wok, add the wine or sherry and cook for 2-3 minutes, carefully turning the fish once.

Lift the fish on to a warmed serving dish and pour the sauce over. Serve hot.

50 FRIED PRAWNS IN BATTER

Preparation time:
about 15 minutes

Cooking time:
about 15 minutes

Serves 4

Calories:
114 per portion

YOU WILL NEED:

225 g/8 oz Pacific prawns
sunflower oil for deep-frying

FOR THE BATTER

½ teaspoon salt

3 tablespoons plain flour

2 tablespoons water

FOR THE DIP

salt

pepper

crushed sesame seeds

Shell the prawns but leave their tails on so that they will be easier to hold.

Beat the egg in a bowl, add the salt and fold in the flour. Stir in the water and beat for 1 minute until light.

Heat the oil in a wok or deep pan until a cube of day-old bread browns in 15 seconds. Dip each prawn in the batter then deep-fry one by one for 2 minutes or until golden. Remove with a slotted spoon and drain on absorbent kitchen paper. Serve hot, with the salt, pepper and sesame seeds mixed together in a shallow saucer as a dip.

▨ COOK'S TIP

In China, a fish weighing less than 1 kg/2 lb is often cooked whole. The fish is slashed on both sides to prevent the skin from bursting when cooking in hot oil, to allow the heat to penetrate quickly and at the same time to help diffuse the flavour of the seasonings.

▨ COOK'S TIP

The quality of this simple batter is its lightness. It should be used soon after preparation. Beat very well to incorporate air into the mixture.

51 TROUT WITH SALTED CABBAGE

Preparation time:	YOU WILL NEED:
15 minutes	2 tablespoons sunflower oil
	1 onion, chopped
Cooking time:	1 x 2.5 cm/1 inch piece fresh root
13 minutes	ginger, peeled and shredded
	4 trout, cleaned
Serves 4	150 ml/ ¼ pint home-made chicken
	stock
Calories:	25 g/1 oz pickled cabbage, chopped
240 per portion	25 g/1 oz canned bamboo shoots,
	drained and sliced
	1 tablespoon light soy sauce
	2 teaspoons Chinese wine or dry sherry
	FOR THE GARNISH
	lemon slices
	fresh coriander leaves

Heat the oil in a wok or deep pan, add the onion and ginger and cook for 1 minute. Add the trout and fry for 1 minute on each side, until browned.

Pour in the stock. Add the cabbage, bamboo shoots, soy sauce and sherry. Cook for 10 minutes over moderate heat, basting the fish occasionally.

Transfer to a warmed serving dish and garnish with lemon slices and coriander leaves. Serve immediately.

▨ COOK'S TIP

Salted cabbage, sometimes called winter pickle, is a mildly salty preserved vegetable sold in jars. If you cannot obtain it, substitute sauerkraut, rinsing it before use to reduce the sharpness.

52 SWEET AND SOUR CARP

Preparation time:	YOU WILL NEED:
20 minutes	15 g/ ½ oz dried wood ears, soaked
	1 x 750 g-1 kg/1½-2lb carp, cleaned
Cooking time:	2 teaspoons salt
about 15 minutes	3 tablespoons flour
	4 tablespoons sunflower oil
Serves 4	2-3 spring onions, shredded
	2 slices fresh root ginger, peeled
Calories:	and shredded
350 per portion	1 garlic clove, chopped
	15 g/ ½ oz bamboo shoots, sliced
	50 g/2 oz water chestnuts, sliced
	1 red pepper, seeded and shredded
	3 tablespoons wine vinegar
	3 tablespoons sugar
	2 tablespoons light soy sauce
	2 tablespoons sake or sherry
	2 teaspoons cornflour
	150 ml/ ¼ pint stock or water

Drain the wood ears and slice them thinly, discarding any hard pieces. Remove the fish fins but leave the head on. Make diagonal slashes along both sides, dry well and rub with 1 teaspoon salt. Coat with the flour. Heat the oil until very hot, reduce the heat and add the fish. Fry for 4-5 minutes on each side until golden and crisp. Drain and keep hot.

Add the wood ears, spring onions, ginger, garlic, bamboo shoots, water chestnuts, red pepper, remaining salt and vinegar. Combine the remaining ingredients, add to the pan and stir until thickened. Pour over the fish to serve.

▨ COOK'S TIP

Carp is best soaked in vinegar and water for 15 minutes before use to bring out the sweet flavour of the firm flesh.

53 CANTONESE SWEET AND SOUR PRAWNS

Preparation time:
10-15 minutes

Cooking time:
15 minutes

Serves 4

Calories:
120 per portion

YOU WILL NEED:
225 g/8 oz Pacific or king prawns
1 egg white
1 tablespoon cornflour
sunflower oil for deep-frying
1 spring onion, finely chopped
2 slices fresh root ginger, peeled
    and finely chopped
FOR THE SAUCE
2 tablespoons sugar
1 tablespoon Chinese wine or
    dry sherry
1 tablespoon light soy sauce
2 teaspoons cornflour
2 tablespoons Chinese stock (see
    recipe 2) or water

Trim the heads, whiskers and legs from the prawns but leave the shells on. Cut each prawn into 2-3 pieces. Mix the egg white and cornflour and use to coat the prawns.

Heat the oil in a wok or deep pan. Before it gets too hot, add the prawns, piece by piece, and fry until golden. Remove with a slotted spoon and drain on absorbent kitchen paper.

Pour off all but 1 tablespoon oil from the wok. Stir-fry the spring onion and ginger for 30 seconds then add the sugar, wine or sherry, soy sauce and vinegar, stirring constantly. When the sugar has dissolved, add the prawns. Mix the cornflour with the stock or water and add to the wok. Stir constantly and serve as soon as the sauce has thickened.

COOK'S TIP

To use chopsticks, put one in the hollow between thumb and forefinger, resting on the third finger, and grasp the other between thumb and forefinger.

54 FILLETS OF SOLE WITH MUSHROOMS

Preparation time:
20 minutes

Cooking time:
5-10 minutes

Serves 3-4

Calories:
300-220 per portion

YOU WILL NEED:
450 g/1 lb sole fillets
1 egg white, lightly beaten
1 tablespoon cornflour
sunflower oil for deep-frying
225 g/8 oz button mushroms, sliced
2-3 spring onions, shredded
1 slice fresh root ginger, shredded
1 teaspoon sugar
1 teaspoon salt
1 tablespoon light soy sauce
1 tablespoon sake or dry sherry
100 ml/4 fl oz fish stock
1 teaspoon sesame oil

Halve the fish fillets if they are large. Place in a bowl and toss in the egg white and cornflour. Heat the oil in a wok or deep pan and deep-fry the fish until golden and crisp; drain on absorbent kitchen paper.

Pour off all but 2 tablespoons of the oil from the wok. Add the mushrooms, spring onions and ginger. Stir-fry for 30 seconds, then add the salt, sugar, soy sauce, sherry and stock. Bring to the boil, add the fish and simmer for 2 minutes. Sprinkle over the sesame oil and serve hot.

COOK'S TIP

Sole features prominently in both French and Chinese cooking as it marries so well with a variety of flavours. There is no need to skin the fillets before cooking as they *keep their shape better with the skin on.*

55 STEAMED WHOLE FISH

Preparation time:
15 minutes, plus
standing

Cooking time:
12 minutes

Serves 4

Calories:
380 per portion

YOU WILL NEED:
3 slices fresh root ginger, peeled
and chopped
2 teaspoons salt
1.25 kg/2½ lb small fish (trout, sole
or mackerel, for example)
3 tablespoons light soy sauce
1½ teaspoons sugar
1 tablespoon wine vinegar
2 tablespoons sunflower oil
2-3 rashers bacon, diced
3-4 large dried Chinese mushrooms,
soaked for 20 minutes (see
Cook's Tip)
4 spring onions, chopped

Combine the ginger and salt and rub over the fish both inside and out. Leave for 30 minutes.

Mix the soy sauce with the sugar, vinegar and oil. Pour this mixture over the fish and leave for 15 minutes.

Transfer the fish to a heatproof dish and spoon over the marinade. Sprinkle with the bacon, mushrooms and spring onions. Place on a rack in a wok containing boiling water or in a steamer and steam vigorously for 12 minutes. The fish is cooked when it will flake easily using chopsticks. Serve hot.

56 PHOENIX-TAIL PRAWNS

Preparation time:
35-45 minutes

Cooking time:
15-20 minutes

Serves 4

Calories:
130 per portion

YOU WILL NEED:
225 g/8 oz Pacific or king prawns
2 tablespoons Chinese wine
1 spring onion, finely chopped
2 slices fresh root ginger, peeled
and finely chopped
sunflower oil for deep-frying
3 egg whites
1 tablespoon cornflour
3 tablespoons plain flour
4 tablespoons breadcrumbs
lettuce leaves
1 tablespoon freshly ground Szechuan
or black pepper

Wash and shell the prawns but leave the tail pieces attached so that they will be easier to hold. Split them in half lengthways and discard the black intestinal vein. Dry the prawns thoroughly and toss them in the salt, wine, spring onion and ginger and 1 teaspoon of the oil.

Place the remaining oil in a wok or deep-fryer over a moderate heat. While it is heating up, beat the egg whites in a bowl until frothy. Fold in the cornflour.

Coat the prawns in the plain flour. Dip each piece in the egg white mixture and then roll them in breadcrumbs. Reduce the heat under the wok and lower the prawns into the oil one by one. Fry in batches until golden, remove with a slotted spoon and drain. Serve on a bed of lettuce leaves.

To make a dip, fry 1 tablespoon salt and the pepper in a dry frying pan for 2-3 minutes over a low heat.

▓ COOK'S TIP

The most common type of Chinese mushroom available is the shiitake, sold dried or fresh. Cloud ears or wood ears are cultivated fungi, often sold dried.

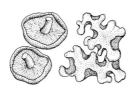

▓ COOK'S TIP

Szechuan peppercorns, despite their name, are not related to true peppercorns. The flavour is pleasantly peppery and best appreciated if briefly dry-fried then *freshly ground. Serve mixed with sea salt as a condiment.*

57 SQUID AND GREEN PEPPERS

Preparation time:	YOU WILL NEED:
20 minutes	225 g/8 oz squid
	sunflower oil for deep-frying
Cooking time:	100 g/4 oz green peppers, seeded
5 minutes	and sliced
	2 slices fresh root ginger, peeled
Serves 4	and thinly sliced
	1 teaspoon salt
Calories:	1 tablespoon light soy sauce
100 per portion	1 teaspoon wine vinegar
	pepper
	1 teaspoon sesame oil

Clean the squid, discarding the head, transparent backbone and ink sac. Peel off the thin skin and cut the flesh into small pieces the size of a matchbox.

In a wok or frying pan heat the oil over a moderate heat and deep-fry the squid for about 30 seconds, stirring with chopsticks to prevent the pieces sticking together.

Pour off all but 1 tablespoon of oil from the wok. Add the ginger, green peppers and squid and stir-fry for 1 minute. Add the salt, soy sauce, vinegar and pepper and stir-fry for 1 minute. Add the sesame oil and serve hot.

58 SOY FISH STEAK

Preparation time:	YOU WILL NEED:
about 15 minutes,	450 g/1 lb fish steak (cod or halibut,
plus marinating	for example)
	½ teaspoon salt
Cooking time:	2 tablespoons sherry
15-20 minutes	4 tablespoons cornflour
	1 egg white, lightly beaten
Serves 4	3 tablespoons sunflower oil
	1 slice fresh root ginger, peeled
Calories:	and finely chopped
312 per portion	2 tablespoons light soy sauce
	2 teaspoons sugar
	100 ml/4 fl oz Chinese stock (see
	recipe 2) or water
	spring onion, to garnish

Cut the fish steak into pieces about the size of a matchbox. Mix together the salt, sherry and 1 tablespoon of the cornflour and marinate the fish in this mixture for about 30 minutes.

Dip the fish pieces in egg white, then in the remaining cornflour.

Heat the oil in a wok or frying pan until hot, then fry the fish pieces until golden, stirring them gently to separate each piece. Add the ginger, soy sauce, sugar and stock or water. Cook for 3-4 minutes, or until the liquid has completely evaporated. Serve hot, garnished with spring onion.

▓ COOK'S TIP

Squid must be cooked quickly or the texture becomes tough. It is ideal for stir-fried dishes such as this, with a sharp contrast of flavours and textures.

After returning the squid to the pan, cook just long enough to blend the flavours.

▓ COOK'S TIP

The rich colour and savoury flavour of soy sauce calls for robust fish with a firm texture. Try this recipe with monkfish, coley or hake.

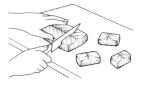

59 FISH AND BEAN CURD CASSEROLE

Preparation time:
20 minutes

Cooking time:
15-20 minutes

Serves 4

Calories:
220 per portion

YOU WILL NEED:
450 g/1 lb firm white fish fillets
1 tablespoon cornflour
2 tablespoons water
1 egg white, lightly beaten
450 g/1 lb firm bean curd or tofu, diced
5-6 Chinese leaves or cos lettuce leaves
3 tablespoons dry sherry
2 tablespoons light soy sauce
1 teaspoon sugar
2 slices fresh root ginger, peeled
3 spring onions, chopped
salt and pepper
300 ml/ ½ pint Chinese stock (see recipe 2)
50 g/2 oz cooked ham, chopped
1 teaspoon sesame oil

Cut the fish into small pieces. Mix the cornflour to a paste with the water and blend with the egg white. Coat the fish with this mixture.

Line a flameproof casserole with the lettuce leaves. Add the bean curd and fish pieces with the sherry, soy sauce, sugar, ginger, spring onions and salt and pepper to taste. Pour over the stock and sprinkle with the ham. Bring to the boil over a moderate heat, cover, reduce the heat and simmer for 15-20 minutes.

Sprinkle with the sesame oil and serve at once.

COOK'S TIP

Since bean curd has little flavour of its own, choose fish with a distinctive taste to accompany it. Salmon is ideal and cod or haddock are good. Add a few cooked prawns, too.

60 STIR-FRIED PRAWNS

Preparation time:
30 minutes

Cooking time:
25 minutes

Serves 4

Calories:
245 per portion

YOU WILL NEED:
450 g/1 lb raw prawns
4 tablespoons sunflower oil
3 slices fresh root ginger, peeled
2 tablespoons cornflour, plus 1 teaspoon
1 teaspoon salt
pepper
1 tablespoon Chinese wine
1 egg white, lightly beaten
225 g/8 oz mangetout, halved
6 canned water chestnuts, drained and thinly sliced
2 tablespoons water
1 teaspoon sesame oil
2 spring onions, finely chopped

Shell the prawns, cut them in half lengthways and remove the black intestinal vein. Wash and dry.

Heat the oil in a wok until it begins to smoke, then add the ginger to flavour the oil. Remove after 30 seconds.

Combine 2 tablespoons cornflour, the salt, pepper, wine and egg white. Toss the prawns in this mixture. Add them to the hot oil, turning and stirring until they change colour. Remove from the wok with a slotted spoon.

Pour off all but 1 tablespoon of oil from the wok. Reheat, then add the mangetout and water chestnuts and stir-fry until they change colour. Return the prawns to the wok. Blend the remaining teaspoon of cornflour with the water and stir it in. Add the sesame oil and spring onions.

COOK'S TIP

There is usually at least one shellfish dish as a Chinese meal and prawns especially lend thenmselves to the subtleties of Chinese cooking. This is one of the prettiest stir-fried recipes, typically displaying a contrast of textures in a single dish.

61 SQUID WITH HERBS

Preparation time:
about 10 minutes

Cooking time:
2 minutes

Serves 4

Calories:
230 per portion

YOU WILL NEED:
1 kg/2 lb baby squid
salt and pepper
4 tablespoons sunflower oil
3-4 cloves garlic, sliced
2 tablespoons freshly chopped
  coriander
1 tablespoon freshly chopped flat-
  leaf parsley
juice of ½ lemon
FOR THE GARNISH
lemon or lime slices
sprigs of herbs

To clean the squid, draw back the rim of the body pouch and pull out the transparent quill. Separate the body from the tentacles and discard the head and ink sac. Peel off the thin skin. Cut the flesh into slices. Season with salt and pepper to taste.

Heat the oil in a wok over gentle heat. Add the garlic slices and cook until browned. Remove with a slotted spoon and discard. Increase the heat. When the oil is hot, add the squid and cook briskly for 1 minute, stirring to prevent the pieces sticking together. Add the coriander, parsley and lemon juice and stir-fry for 30 seconds. Transfer to a warmed serving dish and serve immediately, garnished with lemon or lime slices and tiny bunches of herbs.

62 PRAWNS AND GREEN PEAS

Preparation time:
about 15 minutes,
plus chilling

Cooking time:
5 minutes

Serves 4

Calories:
179 per portion

YOU WILL NEED:
1 egg white, lightly beaten
1 tablespoon cornflour
225 g/8 oz peeled prawns
3 tablespoons sunflower oil
1 slice fresh ginger root, peeled
  and finely chopped
1 spring onion, finely chopped
175 g/6 oz green peas
1½ teaspoons salt
2 teaspoons sugar
1 tablespoon Chinese wine or
  dry sherry
1 teaspoon sesame oil

Mix the egg white and the cornflour and coat the prawns with this mixture. Refrigerate for 20-30 minutes.

Heat the oil in a wok or frying pan over a moderate heat and stir-fry the prawns for 1 minute. Remove with a slotted spoon and drain on absorbent kitchen paper.

Heat the oil remaining in the pan until hot. Add the ginger, onion and green peas and stir-fry for 30 seconds. Add the prawns, salt, sugar and sherry and stir-fry for 1 minute. Add the sesame oil and serve immediately, perhaps with a piquant dip such as the one in recipe 21.

▉COOK'S TIP

Using baby corn ensures a tenderness wich is essential in rapid-fried dishes. This recipe makes an excellent first course or light meal with Vegetable rice (recipe 204) and Fried lettuce (recipe 182).

▉COOK'S TIP

Serve this dish in a lemon basket. Remove 2 segments from 1 side of the lemon, leaving a strip of rind for a handle, and scoop out the flesh with a serrated spoon.

63 CRISPY SKIN FISH

Preparation time:	YOU WILL NEED:
10 minutes, plus standing	675 g/1½ lb small fish (whiting, herring or trout, for example)
	3-4 slices fresh root ginger, peeled and chopped
Cooking time:	1 tablespoon salt
about 10 minutes	1½ tablespoons plain flour
	sunflower oil for deep-frying
Serves 4	
Calories:	
270 per portion	

Slit the fish along the underside. Clean and rinse them thoroughly, leaving the heads and tails intact. Rub the fish inside and out with the ginger and salt. Cover lightly and leave in a cool place for 3 hours. Rub with the flour and leave for a further 30 minutes.

Heat the oil in a wok or deep pan to 180 C/350 F or until a cube of day-old bread browns in 30 seconds. Deep-fry the fish in batches for 3-4 minutes, or until crisp and golden. Drain on absorbent kitchen paper and serve hot.

64 BRAISED FISH WITH SPRING ONIONS AND GINGER

Preparation time:	YOU WILL NEED:
20 minutes	1 x 750 g/1 ¾ lb fish (mullet or bream, for example)
Cooking time:	1 teaspoon salt
about 10 minutes	2 tablespoons flour
	3 tablespoons sunflower oil
Serves 3-4	3-4 spring onions, cut into 2.5 cm/ 1 inch lengths
Calories:	2-3 slices fresh root ginger, shredded
553-415 per portion	FOR THE SAUCE
	2 tablespoons light soy sauce
	2 tablespoons medium or dry sherry
	150 ml/ ¼ pint chicken stock or water
	1 teaspoon cornflour
	pepper

Clean the fish thoroughly, leaving the fins, tail and head on. Slash both sides of the fish diagonally with a sharp knife at 55 mm/ ¼ inch intervals as far as the bone. Rub the fish inside and out with salt, then coat with the flour from head to tail.

Heat the oil in a wok until very hot. Reduce the heat slightly, add the fish and fry for about 2 minutes on each side, turning the fish carefully. Remove from the pan.

Combine the sauce ingredients. Increase the heat and add the spring onions and ginger to the oil remaining in the pan. Stir-fry briefly, add the sauce mixture and replace the fish. Simmer for 2-3 minutes, then transfer the fish to a warmed dish and pour over the sauce. Serve hot.

▨ COOK'S TIP

To ensure a crisp finish, salting the fish before cooking is an essential step as it extracts moisture. As in all deep-frying make sure that the oil reaches the correct temperature and reheat it after cooking each batch.

▨ COOK'S TIP

To scale whole fish such as bream, hold it by the tail end on a board and scrape with a broad-bladed knife or cleaver, working towards the head.

65 STIR-FRIED FISH WITH VEGETABLES

Preparation time:
5 minutes, plus
standing

Cooking time:
5 minutes

Serves 4

Calories:
220 per portion

YOU WILL NEED:
450 g/1 lb cod fillet, skinned and cut
    into wide strips
1 teaspoon salt
1 tablespoon oil
2 rashers back bacon, shredded
50 g/2 oz cooked peas
50 g/2 oz cooked sweetcorn kernels
6 tablespoons Chinese stock (see
    recipe 2) or water
2 teaspoons Chinese wine or dry sherry
2 teaspoons light soy sauce
1 teaspoon sugar
1 teaspoon cornflour
1 teaspoon water
FOR THE GARNISH
lemon slices
spring onions

Sprinkle the fish fillets with the salt and leave to stand for 15 minutes.

Heat the oil in a wok or frying pan over a moderate heat. Add the fish and bacon and stir-fry for 3 minutes. Add the remaining ingredients, except the cornflour and water, and bring to the boil. Blend the cornflour with the water to make a thin paste and stir in to the sauce. Cook for 1 minute.

Serve hot, garnished with lemon slices and spring onions.

66 HOT JUMBO PRAWNS

Preparation time:
10 minutes

Cooking time:
6 minutes

Serves 4

Calories:
370 per portion

YOU WILL NEED:
1 teaspoon very finely chopped fresh
    root ginger
3 spring onions, chopped
12 Pacific prawns, peeled
3 tablespoons self-raising flour
pinch of salt
½-1 teaspoon chilli powder
½ teaspoon paprika
3 teaspoons dry sherry
1 egg, beaten
1 tablespoon freshly chopped coriander
sunflower oil for deep-frying
FOR THE GARNISH
tomato roses
coriander leaves

Mix together the ginger, spring onions and prawns. Place the flour, salt, chilli powder to taste and paprika in a bowl. Add the sherry and egg and beat to a smooth batter. Fold in the coriander and the prawn mixture.

Heat the oil to 160 C/325°F or until a cube of day-old bread browns in 45 seconds. Deep-fry half the battered prawns for 2-3 minutes until golden. Drain on absorbent kitchen paper and keep hot while frying the remainder.

Arrange on a warmed serving dish. Garnish with coriander leaves and tomato roses, made by paring the skin from a tomato in a single piece and curling it into a circle.

▓ COOK'S TIP

This recipe can be varied. Use different kinds of fish and vegetables according to season and availability, making sure that the ingredients are sliced to a similar size.

▓ COOK'S TIP

Leave the tails on the prawns when you prepare them so that guests can hold them when eating. The thick batter ensures that the prawns remain moist and tender.

67 CHINESE STEAMED TROUT

Preparation time:
10 minutes

Cooking time:
15 minutes

Serves 4

Calories:
350 per portion

YOU WILL NEED:
1 tablespoon sesame oil
1 tablespoon light soy sauce
1 tablespoon dry sherry
2 rainbow trout, about 1 kg/2 lb total
   weight, cleaned
4 garlic cloves, sliced
6 spring onions, shredded
1 x 5 cm/2 inch piece fresh root ginger,
   peeled and shredded
2 tablespoons dry white vermouth
2 tablespoons sunflower oil

Mix together the sesame oil, soy sauce and sherry and use to brush the inside and skin of the fish. Mix together the garlic, spring onions and ginger and place a quarter of this mixture inside each fish.

Place the fish on a heatproof plate, scatter over the remaining garlic mixture and pour over the vermouth and oil. Put the plate in a wok or steamer and steam vigorously for 15 minutes, or until the fish are tender.

Arrange on a warmed serving dish, pour over the juices and serve at once.

68 STEAMED SWEET AND SOUR FISH

Preparation time:
10 minutes

Cooking time:
12-15 minutes

Serves 4

Calories:
150 per portion

YOU WILL NEED:
1 large whole plaice, cleaned
salt
2 x 2.5 cm/1 inch pieces fresh
   root ginger, shredded
3 spring onions, sliced
FOR THE SAUCE
150 ml/ ¼ pint fish or chicken stock
1 tablespoon light soy sauce
1 tablespoon sugar
1 tablespoon wine vinegar
1 tablespoon Chinese wine or
   dry sherry
1 tablespoon tomato purée
1 teaspoon chilli sauce
pinch of salt
1 tablespoon cornflour
2 tablespoons water

Score the fish by making 3 diagonal cuts on each side. Rub the fish with salt and sprinkle with the ginger and spring onions. Place on an ovenproof plate and steam for 12-15 minutes until tender.

To make the sauce, combine all the ingredients except the cornflour and water in a small pan. Bring to the boil and cook for 1 minute. Blend the cornflour with the water and stir this paste into the sauce. Cook, still stirring, until the sauce has thickened. Carefully lift the plaice on to a serving dish and spoon over the sauce. Serve hot.

▨ COOK'S TIP

Steaming is an excellent method for cooking all fish as it preserves the delicate flavour. For fish that require careful handling such as trout, it is particularly *recommended. The flesh stays perfectly intact during the cooking process.*

▨ COOK'S TIP

To serve whole plaice, make a cut down the centre, then down one side, and lift off the fillet. Repeat on the other side. Snip the bone at head and tail and remove it.

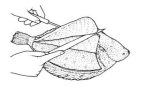

69   SPICY FISH WITH VEGETABLES

Preparation time:
20 minutes

Cooking time:
10-15 minutes

Serves 4

Calories:
170 per portion

YOU WILL NEED:
600 ml/1 pint water
1 teaspoon chilli powder
1 tablespoon chilli sauce
1 teaspoon salt
450 g/1 lb cod fillets, cubed
20 shellfish (cooked mussels, prawns
*   and scallops, for example)*
1 onion, cut into 8 pieces
20 button mushrooms
1 red pepper, cut into 8 pieces
1 garlic clove, crushed
4 spring onions, chopped
1 courgette, cut into 8 pieces
FOR THE GARNISH
cress
enokitake mushrooms (optional)

Place the water, chilli powder, chill sauce and salt in a pan and bring to the boil. Add the fish, shelled shellfish, onion, mushrooms, red pepper and garlic. Bring back to the boil. Add the spring onions and courgette and simmer for 10 minutes or until just cooked.

Divide between the 4 serving bowls and serve at once, sprinkled with the cress and enokitake mushrooms (if used).

70   SOY-BRAISED COD STEAKS

Preparation time:
15 minutes

Cooking time:
about 12 minutes

Serves 4

Calories:
260 per portion

YOU WILL NEED:
50 g/2 oz lard
3-4 spring onions, chopped
2-3 slices fresh root ginger, peeled
*   and chopped*
450 g/1 lb cod steaks, quartered
2 tablespoons Chinese wine or sherry
2 tablespoons light soy sauce
1 tablespoon sugar
125 ml/4½ fl oz water
1 tablespoon cornflour
1 teaspoon sesame oil
shredded spring onion, to garnish

Melt the lard in a pan over a high heat. Add the spring onions and ginger and stir-fry for a few seconds. Add the fish pieces and stir very gently to separate them. Add the wine or sherry and bring to the boil. Stir in the soy sauce, sugar and 100 ml/ 4 fl oz of the water. Simmer for about 10 minutes.

Blend the remaining water with the cornflour. Add this mixture to the pan and stir until thickened. Add the sesame oil and serve hot, garnished with shredded spring onion.

▓ COOK'S TIP

When making this colourful stew, keep the liquid at simmering point so that the texture of the fish remains tender, and the vegetables crunchy.

▓ COOK'S TIP

Lard is frequently used in Chinese cooking to give a smoothness to savoury sauces. This recipe works well with halibut, which can be on the dry side and *benefits from being cooked in liquid.*

71 PRAWNS IN CHILLI SAUCE

Preparation time:
6 minutes

Cooking time:
6 minutes

Serves 4

Calories:
140 per portion

YOU WILL NEED:
1 tablespoon sunflower oil
3 spring onions, chopped
2 teaspoons freshly chopped
    root ginger
225 g/8 oz peeled prawns
100 g/4 oz mangetout
½ teaspoon chilli powder
1 teaspoon tomato purée
¼ teaspoon salt
½ teaspoon sugar
1 tablespoon Chinese wine or
    dry sherry
½ teaspoon sesame oil
whole unshelled prawns, to garnish

Heat the oil in a wok or deep frying pan over a moderate heat. Add the spring onions and ginger and stir-fry for 30 seconds. Add the prawns, mangetout, chilli powder, tomato purée, salt, sugar and wine or sherry and stir-fry briskly for 5 minutes.

Sprinkle over the sesame oil and serve at once, garnished with whole prawns.

72 PRAWNS WITH ASPARAGUS

Preparation time:
5 minutes, plus
marinating

Cooking time:
4 minutes

Serves 4

Calories:
200 per portion

YOU WILL NEED:
175 g/6 oz fresh asparagus, cut into
    2.5 cm/1 inch pieces
½ teaspoon salt
4 tablespoons Chinese wine or
    dry sherry
1 teaspoon light soy sauce
450 g/1 lb peeled prawns
2 tablespoons sunflower oil
2 garlic cloves, thinly sliced
2 teaspoons freshly chopped
    root ginger
4 spring onions, chopped

Blanch the asparagus in boiling salted water for 2 minutes. Drain well and set aside.

Mix the wine or sherry with the soy sauce. Stir in the prawns and leave to marinate for 15 minutes.

Heat the oil in a wok or deep frying pan and quickly stir-fry the garlic, ginger and half the spring onions. Add the prawns and marinade, and the asparagus, and stir-fry for 1-2 minutes, until the ingredients are hot. Sprinkle with the remaining spring onions and serve at once.

▨ COOK'S TIP

Chillies are much used in the cooking of Szechuan. Offset their sharp, hot flavours with a selection of refreshing vegetable dishes and a bowl of plain rice.

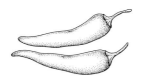

▨ COOK'S TIP

To prepare asparagus for this quick-to-cook dish, cut off all the woody stem so that only the tender stalk remains. Be careful not to overcook the delicate tips.

73 STIR-FRIED SQUID WITH VEGETABLES

Preparation time:
30 minutes

Cooking time:
about 10 minutes

Serves 4

Calories:
270 per portion

YOU WILL NEED:

400 g/14 oz squid, cleaned (see recipe 7)

2 slices fresh root ginger, peeled and chopped

1 tablespoon sake or dry sherry

1 tablespoon cornflour

15 g/ ½ oz dried wood ears, soaked for 20 minutes

4 tablespoons sunflower oil

2 spring onions, chopped

225 g/8 oz cauliflower or broccoli florets

2 carrots, cut in diamond-shapes

teaspoon salt

1 teaspoon sugar

1 teaspoon sesame oil

Cut the prepared squid into rings and thin slices. Place in a bowl with half the ginger, the sake or sherry and cornflour. Mix well and stand 20 minutes. Meanwhile, drain the wood ears and break into small pieces, discarding the hard parts.

Heat 2 tablespoons of the oil in a wok or frying pan. Add the spring onions and remaining ginger, the cauliflower or broccoli, carrots and wood ears. Stir, then add the salt and sugar. Cook until the vegetables are tender. Remove from the wok with a slotted spoon and drain.

Heat the remaining oil in the wok, add the squid and stir-fry for about 1 minute. Return the vegetables to the wok, add the sesame oil and stir briefly. Serve hot.

▓ COOK'S TIP

Marinating tenderizes food as well as giving it flavour, so this is a good recipe for large squid which may not be perfectly tender.

74 PRAWN CUTLETS

Preparation time:
10 minutes

Cooking time:
2-3 minutes

Serves 2

Calories:
230 per portion

YOU WILL NEED:

8 Dublin Bay or large king prawns in their shells

1 tablespoon dry sherry

1 egg, beaten

2 tablespoons cornflour

sunflower oil for deep-frying

fresh coriander leaves, to garnish

Wash the prawns. Holding them firmly by the tails, remove the shell, leaving the tail shell intact. Cut the prawns in half lengthways almost to the tail and remove the black intestinal vein. Flatten the prawns. Sprinkle them with the sherry, dip in the egg and coat in the cornflour. Repeat the coating.

Heat the oil to 180 C/350 F or until a cube of day-old bread browns in 30 seconds. Deep-fry the prawns for 2-3 minutes. Drain on absorbent kitchen paper and serve at once, garnished with fresh coriander. The prawn cutlets may be served with a satay sauce (see Cook's Tip).

▓ COOK'S TIP

For a satay sauce, blend 1 small onion to a purée with 1 teaspoon of chilli powder, 1 teaspoon of shrimp paste and a pinch of salt. Fry in hot oil for 3 minutes then add 1 tablespoon of lemon juice, 1 tablespoon of sugar, 175 g/6 oz finely chopped unsalted peanuts and enough water to give a thick, smooth consistency. Stir well; serve.

75 BRAISED FISH WITH BLACK BEAN SAUCE

Preparation time:
20 minutes

Cooking time:
10-15 minutes

Serves 4

Calories:
260 per portion

YOU WILL NEED:
3 tablespoons salted black beans
2 tablespoons oil
2 spring onions, chopped
1 x 2.5cm/1inch piece fresh root ginger,
   peeled and chopped
1 small red pepper, cored, seeded
   and chopped
2 celery sticks, chopped
2 tablespoons light soy sauce
2 tablespoons dry sherry
4 x 150 g/5 oz cod or haddock cutlets
shredded spring onion, to garnish

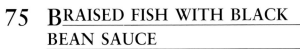

Soak the black beans in warm water for 10 minutes. Drain.

Heat the oil in a wok or deep frying pan. Add the spring onions, ginger, red pepper and celery and stir-fry for 1 minute. Stir in the soy sauce and sherry. Place the fish on top of the vegetables and simmer for 5-10 minutes, until almost tender. Timing will depend upon the thickness of the fish. Spoon over the black beans and cook for 2 minutes.

Arrange the fish on a warmed serving dish and spoon the sauce over. Serve hot, garnished with shredded spring onion.

76 SOLE WITH SATAY SAUCE

Preparation time:
35 minutes

Cooking time:
20 minutes

Serves 4

Calories:
750 per portion

YOU WILL NEED:
1 teaspoon each of coriander, cumin
   and fennel seeds, crushed
2 garlic cloves, crushed
100 g/4 oz crunchy peanut butter
1 teaspoon dark soft brown sugar
2 fresh green chillies, chopped
150 g/5 oz creamed coconut
450 ml/ ¾ pint water
3 tablespoons lemon juice
25 g/1 oz butter
1 shallot, finely chopped
1 tablespoon each of chopped chives,
   tarragon and parsley
grated rind of ½ lemon
8 Dover or lemon sole fillets
1 egg, beaten
4-5 tablespoons fresh breadcrumbs
sunflower oil for deep-frying

To make the sauce, heat a wok, add the seeds and stir-fry 2 minutes. Add the garlic, peanut butter, sugar and chillies. Combine the creamed coconut with the water and stir it in. Cook gently for 7-8 minutes. Stir in the lemon juice.

Melt the butter in a pan, add the shallot and cook for 1 minute. Stir in the herbs and lemon rind. Cool slightly, then pour this mixture over the fish fillets. Roll up each one and secure with wooden cocktail sticks. Dip in the egg, coat in breadcrumbs, and deep-fry in hot oil for 4-5 minutes until golden. Drain and serve with the sauce handed separately.

▒ COOK'S TIP

This rich, colourful mixture of vegetables makes a hearty dish with steaks of firm white fish. Because black beans are extremely salty they will keep indefinitely but must always *be soaked before being used in cooking.*

▒ COOK'S TIP

Creamed coconut is sold in blocks which should be softened in boiling water before use. Coconut powder, mixed to a paste with water, is an acceptable substitute.

POULTRY & GAME

China has given the world some of the most famous poultry dishes – Peking duck, for example – and some of the most popular. The regional cooking of China boasts innumerable ideas for chicken, from subtle Peppered smoked chicken from Szechuan to tangy Ginger chicken from Canton.

77 CHICKEN IN SESAME SAUCE

Preparation time:
15 minutes, plus
marinating

Cooking time:
3-5 minutes

Serves 4-6

Calories:
500-340 per portion

YOU WILL NEED:
*450 g/1 lb boneless chicken breast,
    skin removed*
1 tablespoon sunflower oil
100 g/4 oz unsalted cashew nuts
*75 g/3 oz canned straw mushrooms,
    drained and halved*
FOR THE MARINADE
3 spring onions, chopped
3 tablespoons light soy sauce
2 tablespoons hot pepper oil
2 tablespoons sesame oil
1 tablespoon sesame seed paste (tahini)
*1 teaspoon ground Szechuan
    peppercorns*

Cut the chicken into cubes. Put all the marinade ingredients into a bowl and add the chicken, turning to coat the pieces thoroughly. Leave to marinate for 30 minutes.

Meanwhile, heat the oil in a wok or frying pan. Add the cashew nuts and fry them until golden. Drain on absorbent kitchen paper.

Add the chicken and marinade to the wok and stir-fry for 2 minutes. Add the mushrooms and cook for a further minute. Pile the mixture into a warmed serving dish and sprinkle with the nuts. Serve at once.

78 GINGER CHICKEN

Preparation time:
10 minutes, plus
standing

Cooking time:
about 10 minutes

Serves 4

Calories:
370 per portion

YOU WILL NEED:
*675 g/1½ lb chicken breasts, cut into
    finger-sized pieces*
1 teaspoon sugar
salt and pepper
4 tablespoons sesame oil
*1 × 10 cm/4 inch piece fresh root
    ginger, peeled and finely sliced*
75-100 ml/3-4 fl oz water
100 g/4 oz button mushrooms
2 tablespoons brandy
*2 teaspoons cornflour, blended with
    3 tablespoons water*
1 teaspoon light soy sauce

Sprinkle the chicken with the sugar and leave to stand for 20-30 minutes. Season with salt and pepper.

Heat the oil and fry the ginger for 1 minute. Add the chicken pieces and cook for 3 minutes. Stir in the water and mushrooms. Cover and cook for a further 5 minutes, or until the chicken is tender.

Add the brandy, cornflour mixture and soy sauce. Bring to the boil, stirring, until thickened. Serve at once.

■ COOK'S TIP

The combination of sesame oil and sesame seed paste gives this dish a wonderfully nutty flavour and warm colour. Do not cook sesame oil for very long as it burns very easily. If you wish, add a little more oil immediately before serving, trickling it over the dish to give a gleaming finish.

■ COOK'S TIP

Fresh ginger keeps in the freezer, wrapped in cling film, or in the refrigerator in a tightly sealed jar of dry sherry. Ground ginger is not an acceptable substitute.

79 STIR-FRIED CHICKEN WITH CORN AND MUSHROOMS

Preparation time:
15 minutes, plus soaking

Cooking time:
30 minutes

Serves 4

Calories:
271 per portion

YOU WILL NEED:
25 g/1 oz dried shiitake mushrooms
5 tablespoons sunflower oil
2 garlic cloves, crushed
225 g/8 oz boneless chicken breast,
    cut into strips
50 g/2 oz baby corn cobs, blanched
175 ml/6 fl oz chicken stock
1 tablespoon nam pla (fish sauce)
generous pinch of salt
generous pinch of sugar
½ tablespoon cornflour
2 tablespoons water

Soak the dried mushrooms in warm water to cover for 15 minutes. Discard the stems and cut the caps into quarters.

Heat the oil in a wok or large frying pan. Add the garlic and cook over moderate heat until golden. Add the chicken and stir-fry for 10 minutes. Lift out and set aside.

Add the mushrooms and baby corn to the oil remaining in the wok. Stir-fry for 1-2 minutes. Stir in the chicken stock and bring to the boil. Reduce the heat, return the chicken to the wok and season with nam pla, salt and sugar. Simmer for 10 minutes or until the chicken is tender and the liquid is reduced by about half.

Mix the cornflour with the water to make a thin paste. Add to the chicken mixture and cook, stirring constantly,until the sauce thickens. Serve immediately.

■COOK'S TIP

For the best results, choose chickens that are free-range and preferably corn-fed. Chinese and South-East Asian chickens are smaller than those bred in the West, *but they have a superb flavour.*

80 STEWED CHICKEN WITH CHESTNUTS

Preparation time:
40 minutes, plus marinating

Cooking time:
about 1 hour

Serves 4

Calories:
565 per portion

YOU WILL NEED:
450 g/1 lb chestnuts, peeled
    and skinned (see method)
6 tablespoons light soy sauce
1 tablespoon Chinese wine or
    dry sherry
1 x 1 kg/2 lb chicken, boned and cut
    into 4 cm/1½ inch pieces
2 tablespoons sunflower oil
2 slices fresh root ginger, peeled
    and chopped
4 spring onions, chopped
450 ml/ ¾ pint water
1 tablespoon sugar

To peel chestnuts, first remove a thin strip from one side. Place in a pan of cold water, bring to the boil and boil for 1 minute. Remove from the heat. Work with 2 or 3 at a time, leaving the remainder in the hot water. Peel off the shells and then the thin inner skins.

Mix together the soy sauce and wine or sherry in a dish and add the chicken. Leave to marinate for 15 minutes, turning from time to time.

Heat the oil in a large pan. Add the chicken mixture, ginger and half of the spring onions; stir-fry until the chicken is golden. Add the chestnuts, water and sugar. Bring to the boil, cover and simmer for 40 minutes or until tender. Serve hot, garnished with the remaining spring onions.

■COOK'S TIP

When peeling chestnuts, do all the work while the chestnuts are still warm. The skins will harden again as the chestnuts cool.

81 CHICKEN WITH SESAME SEEDS

Preparation time:
5 minutes, plus
marinating

Cooking time:
4 minutes

Serves 4

Calories:
230 per portion

YOU WILL NEED:
350 g/12 oz boneless chicken, skin
    removed
1 egg white, lightly beaten
½ teaspoon salt
2 teaspoons cornflour
2 tablespoons white sesame seeds
2 tablespoons sunflower oil
1 tablespoon dark soy sauce
1 tablespoon wine vinegar
½ teaspoon chilli bean sauce
½ teaspoon sesame oil
1 tablespoon Chinese wine or
    dry sherry
½ teaspoon roasted Szechuan
    peppercorns
4 spring onions, chopped

Cut the chicken into 7.5 cm/3 inch long shreds. Mix the egg white, salt and cornflour, toss in the chicken and mix well. Leave to stand for 15 minutes.

Fry the sesame seeds in a wok or pan in a little hot oil until golden. Remove and set aside.

Heat the remaining oil in the wok, add the chicken and stir-fry for 1 minute. Remove with a slotted spoon. Add the soy sauce, vinegar, chilli bean sauce, sesame oil, wine or sherry and peppercorns and bring to the boil. Replace the chicken, add the spring onions and cook for 2 minutes, stirring constantly. Sprinkle with the sesame seeds and serve at while still hot.

■ COOK'S TIP

*Sesame seeds have a nutty
and aromatic taste. The seeds
can be used raw or toasted.
To toast them, fry in a dry
wok until they start to jump
and turn golden brown.*

82 CHICKEN WITH WALNUTS

Preparation time:
10 minutes

Cooking time:
5 minutes

Serves 2-3

Calories:
634-425 per portion

YOU WILL NEED:
275-350 g/10-12 oz boneless chicken
    breast, skinned and diced
½ teaspoon salt
1 egg white, lightly beaten
1 tablespoon cornflour, plus 1 teaspoon
1 green pepper, cored and seeded
50 g/2 oz shelled walnuts
4 tablespoons sunflower oil
2 spring onions, cut into short sections
2 slices fresh root ginger, peeled
3-4 dried red chillies, sliced
1 tablespoon yellow or black bean
    sauce
1 teaspoon sugar
2 tablespoons Chinese wine or
    dry sherry
1 tablespoon water

Mix the chicken first with the salt, then the egg white and finally 1 tablespoon cornflour. Dice the green pepper and walnuts the same size as the chicken.

Heat the oil in a hot wok, add the chicken and stir-fry for a few seconds until the flesh turns white. Remove from the oil and set aside. Add the spring onions, ginger, chillies and walnuts to the oil. Stir in the bean sauce, then the green pepper. Replace the chicken, stir-fry for 1 minute, and add the sugar and wine. Cook for 1 minute.

Combine the remaining cornflour with the water and add to the wok, stirring until the sauce is thickened. Serve hot.

■ COOK'S TIP

*Whole dried red chillies give
heat to this popular dish
from Szechuan. The amount
of chillies can be adjusted
according to taste. If the
chillies are left whole the*
    *dish will be less hot, as the
seeds are the hottest part.
Almonds, cashew nuts or
peanuts can be used instead
of walnuts.*

83 CASHEW CHICKEN

Preparation time:
5 minutes

Cooking time:
3 minutes

Serves 4

Calories:
420 per portion

YOU WILL NEED:
350 g/12 oz boneless chicken
1 egg white, lightly beaten
4 tablespoons Chinese wine or
   dry sherry
2 teaspoons cornflour
3 tablespoons sunflower oil
4 spring onions, chopped
2 garlic cloves, chopped
1 x 2.5 cm/1 inch piece fresh root
   ginger, peeled and finely chopped
1 tablespoon light soy sauce
100 g/4 oz unsalted cashew nuts

Cut the chicken into 1 cm/ ½ inch cubes. Mix the egg white, half the wine or sherry and the cornflour together. Place the chicken cubes in this mixture and toss until evenly coated.

Heat the oil in a wok. Add the spring onions, garlic and ginger and stir-fry for 30 seconds. Add the chicken and cook for 2 minutes. Pour in the remaining wine or sherry and the soy sauce and stir well. Add the cashew nuts and cook for a further 30 seconds. Serve at once.

84 STEAMED CHICKEN WITH MUSHROOMS

Preparation time:
10-15 minutes, plus
soaking

Cooking time:
20 minutes

Serves 4

Calories:
307 per portion

YOU WILL NEED:
750 g/1¾ lb boneless chicken, skin
   removed
1 teaspoon salt
1 teaspoon sugar
1 tablespoon Chinese wine or
   dry sherry
1 teaspoon cornflour
3-4 dried Chinese mushrooms
2 slices fresh root ginger, peeled
1 teaspoon sunflower oil
freshly ground Szechuan or black
   pepper
1 teaspoon sesame oil
spring onion tassels, to garnish (see
   recipe 33)

Cut the chicken into bite-sized pieces and mix with the salt, sugar, wine or sherry and cornflour. Soak the mushrooms in warm water for 15-20 minutes, squeeze dry and discard the hard stalks.

Thinly shred the mushrooms and ginger. Grease a heatproof plate with the oil. Place the chicken pieces on the plate with the shredded mushrooms and ginger scattered on top. Add the ground pepper and the sesame oil.

Place the chicken dish in a steamer and steam vigorously for 20 minutes. Serve hot.

■ COOK'S TIP

Cashew nuts are highly nutritious, with 21 per cent protein and 22 per cent carbohydrate content. They have considerable vitamin and mineral value.

■ COOK'S TIP

This dish is best using the breast and thighs of a young, free-range chicken. The distinctive, delicate flavours and tender texture are retained by steaming.

85 STEAMED CHICKEN WITH CHINESE CABBAGE

Preparation time:
10 minutes

Cooking time:
2 hours 15 minutes

Serves 4-6

Calories:
399-266 per portion

YOU WILL NEED:
1 x 1.5 kg/3½ lb chicken
2 teaspoons salt
6-8 dried shiitake mushrooms
750 g/1½ lb Chinese cabbage
5 slices fresh root ginger, peeled
2 chicken stock cubes

Bring a large saucepan of water to the boil. Add the salt and immerse the chicken in the water. Skim off all scum that rises to the surface and boil for 5-6 minutes. Drain the chicken.

Soak the mushrooms in boiling water and leave to stand for 20 minutes. Drain and discard the stems. Cut the cabbage into 5 cm/2 inch slices.

Place the mushroom caps and ginger in a large, deep, heatproof bowl. Put the chicken on top of the vegetables and pour in just enough water to cover it. Cover the top of the bowl tightly with kitchen foil. Place the bowl in a large saucepan of water, which should not come more than half-way up the sides of the bowl. Bring the water to the boil, then simmer for 1 hour, topping up with boiling water if necessary.

Lift out the chicken. Place the sliced cabbage in the bottom of the bowl and sprinkle with the crumbled stock cubes. Replace the chicken. Tightly cover the bowl again with foil and simmer gently for 1 more hour. Arrange the vegetables and chicken on a warmed platter to serve.

■ COOK'S TIP

This cooking method, akin to double-boiling, is a favourite in China because it produces a very pure, true flavour, which calls for a chicken of good quality — preferably free range. Serve with plain boiled rice.

86 LEMON CHICKEN

Preparation time:
25 minutes

Cooking time:
about 5 minutes

Serves 4

Calories:
550 per portion

YOU WILL NEED:
1 x 1.5 kg/3 ½ lb chicken, boned and cubed
salt and pepper
5 tablespoons sunflower oil
5-6 dried Chinese mushrooms
15 g/ ½ oz lard
4 slices fresh root ginger, chopped
1 red pepper, cored, seeded and sliced
shredded rind of 2 lemons
5 spring onions, sliced
4 tablespoons Chinese wine or dry sherry
1½ teaspoons sugar
2 tablepoons light soy sauce
1 teaspoon cornflour
1 tablespoon water
1-2 tablespoons lemon juice

Rub the chicken with 1½ teaspoons salt, pepper to taste and 1½ tablespoons of the oil. Heat the remaining oil in a pan until hot. Add the chicken and stir-fry for 2 minutes. Remove the chicken from the pan and keep warm.

Soak the mushrooms in boiling water and leave to stand for 20 minutes. Drain, discard the stems and shred the caps.

Melt the lard in the pan. Add the ginger, pepper and mushrooms and stir-fry 1 minute. Add the lemon rind and spring onions. Stir-fry 30 seconds. Sprinkle in the wine, sugar and soy sauce. Mix the cornflour with the water and add to the pan. Stir for 1 minute and sprinkle in the lemon juice.

■ COOK'S TIP

The addition of red pepper makes this great mix of lemon and chicken very high in vitamin C. Serve it with a simple noodle dish and spring rolls.

87 SPICY CHICKEN AND PEANUTS

Preparation time:
5 minutes

Cooking time:
3½ minutes

Serves 4

Calories:
380 per portion

YOU WILL NEED:
100 g/4 oz unsalted peanuts
350 g/12 oz boneless chicken, skin
    removed
2 tablespoons sunflower oil
1 dried red chilli
2 tablespoons Chinese wine or
    dry sherry
1 tablespoon dark soy sauce
pinch of sugar
1 garlic clove, crushed
2 spring onions, chopped
1 x 2.5 cm/1 inch piece fresh root
    ginger, peeled and finely chopped
1 teaspoon wine vinegar
2 teaspoons sesame oil

Immerse the peanuts in boiling water for about 2 minutes. Drain and remove the skins, then dry well. Cut the chicken into cubes.

Heat the oil in a wok or frying pan. Crumble in the chilli, add the chicken pieces and peanuts and stir-fry for 1 minute. Remove from the wok. Place the wine or sherry, soy sauce, sugar, garlic, spring onions, ginger and vinegar in the wok. Bring to the boil, then simmer for 30 seconds. Return the chicken, chilli and peanuts to the wok and cook for 2 minutes. Sprinkle over the sesame oil and serve at once, while very hot.

■ COOK'S TIP

There are many versions of this classic Chinese dish, better known as Gongbao Chicken. Chicken breast meat is recommended for tenderness in contrast to the crunchy texture of the nuts. Vary the amount of chilli if you wish, but use enough to give the dish some 'bite'.

88 CHICKEN WITH SHRIMP SAUCE

Preparation time:
30 minutes

Cooking time:
about 40 minutes

Serves 4

Calories:
440 per portion

YOU WILL NEED:
1.5 kg/3½ lb chicken joints
1 onion, quartered
4 garlic cloves, peeled
1 x 2.5 cm/1 inch piece fresh root
    ginger, peeled and chopped
3 fresh red chillies, seeded and
    quartered
1 tablespoon water
3 tablespoons sunflower oil
1 teaspoon turmeric
1 teaspoon pepper
½ teaspoon dried shrimp paste
½ teaspoon laos powder
2 strips lemon rind
2 teaspoons nam pla (fish sauce)
1½ teaspoons salt
30 ml/½ pint coconut milk
1 tablespoon sugar
2 tablespoons lemon juice

Cut the chicken into 4cm/1½ inch pieces. Purée the onion, garlic, ginger and chillies with the water.

Heat the oil in a wok and fry the onion mixture for 3-4 minutes. Add the turmeric, pepper, shrimp paste and laos powder and cook for 1 minute. Add the lemon rind, nam pla, salt and chicken pieces and stir-fry until turning brown. Add the coconut milk and sugar and simmer, covered, for 30 minutes or until tender. Stir in the lemon juice and serve.

■ COOK'S TIP

Laos powder is derived from galangal or lengkuas, a relative of ginger. If using laos powder instead of the fresh root, 1 teaspoon equals 1cm/½ inch piece of root.

89 CHICKEN WINGS ASSEMBLY

Preparation time:
10-15 minutes, plus marinating

Cooking time:
25-30 minutes

Serves 4

Calories:
420 per portion

YOU WILL NEED:
12 chicken wings
¼ teaspoon salt
1 tablespoon sugar
2 tablespoons soy sauce
2 tablespoons Chinese wine or
      dry sherry
1 tablespoon cornflour
2 tablespoons sunflower oil
1 garlic clove, crushed
3 spring onions, cut into short lengths
3-4 tablespoons Chinese stock (see
      recipe 2) or water
1 teaspoon sesame oil

Trim off and discard the tips of the wings (they can be used for stock) and cut the remainder of the wings into 2 pieces by breaking them at the joint. Mix them with the salt, sugar, soy sauce, wine or sherry and cornflour. Marinate for about 10 minutes, turning them once or twice.

Heat the oil in a preheated wok or frying pan. Stir-fry the chicken wings for about 1 minute, or until they start to turn brown, then lift them out with a slotted spoon. Add the crushed garlic and spring onions to the wok to flavour the oil, then add the chicken wings and a little of the stock or water. Stir, then cover and cook over a fairly high heat for about 5 minutes. Add a little more stock if necessary and stir so that the chicken pieces do not stick.

Cover and cook a further 5-10 minutes, until the sauce is absorbed. Add the sesame oil, stir and serve immediately.

◾ COOK'S TIP

Serve this dish as part of a varied menu that includes one steamed dish, one braised dish, rice or noodles and both cooked and pickled vegetables. Chicken wings
are also useful for buffet parties as they are eaten with the fingers.

90 BRAISED CHICKEN WINGS

Preparation time:
15 minutes

Cooking time:
about 10 minutes

Serves 4

Calories:
400 per portion

YOU WILL NEED:
12 chicken wings
4 dried Chinese mushrooms
2 tablespoons sunflower oil
2 spring onions, finely chopped
2 slices fresh root ginger, peeled
      and chopped
2 tablespoons light soy sauce
2 tablespoons sake or dry sherry
1 tablespoon sugar
½ teaspoon 5-spice powder
350 ml/12 fl oz water
175 g/6 oz bamboo shoots, cubed
2 teaspoons cornflour
1 tablespoon water

Remove the tips of the chicken wings (they can be used for stock) and break each wing into 2 pieces at the joint.

Soak the mushrooms in boiling water for 20 minutes. Drain, discard the stems and slice the caps.

Heat the oil in a wok until it is smoking. Add the spring onions and ginger, then the chicken wings. Stir-fry until the chicken changes colour, then add the soy sauce, sake or sherry, sugar, 5-spice powder and water. Reduce the heat and cook until the liquid is reduced by about half. Add the mushrooms and bamboo shoots and continue to cook until nearly all the juices have evaporated. Remove the bamboo chunks, rinse and arrange around the edge of a serving dish.

Make a paste of the cornflour and water and add to the wok. Stir to thicken, then transfer to the serving dish.

◾ COOK'S TIP

If you do not wish to use a whole can of bamboo shoots, they will keep in the refrigerator for up to 10 days if put in a jar of fresh water which is changed every day.

91 CHICKEN IN FOIL

Preparation time:	YOU WILL NEED:
15 minutes, plus marinating	1 tablespoon light soy sauce
	1 tablespoon Chinese wine or dry sherry
Cooking time:	1 tablespoon sesame oil
10-12 minutes	450 g/1 lb boneless chicken breast, skin removed
	oil for brushing
Serves 4-6	4 spring onions, each cut into 4 pieces
	1 × 2.5 cm/1 inch piece fresh root ginger, peeled and shredded
Calories:	
190-125 per portion	1 celery stick, shredded

Mix the soy sauce, wine or sherry and sesame oil together. Cut the chicken into 16 even pieces and toss them in this mixture. Leave to marinate for 15-20 minutes.

Cut out 16 pieces of kitchen foil large enough to enclose the chicken pieces generously. Brush the foil with oil, place a piece of chicken in the centre of each piece and top with a piece of spring onion, some ginger and celery. Fold over the foil to enclose the chicken and seal the edges well. Place in a steamer and steam vigorously for 10-12 minutes. Serve hot, wrapped in foil, for guests to open their own packages.

92 CHICKEN CUBES WITH CELERY

Preparation time:	YOU WILL NEED:
15-20 minutes	2 boneless chicken breasts, skin removed
Cooking time:	½ teaspoon salt
4 minutes	1 egg white, lightly beaten
	1 tablespoon cornflour
Serves 4	1 small head celery
	4 tablespoons oil
Calories:	1 tablespoon Chinese wine or dry sherry
250 per portion	1 tablespoon light soy sauce
	1 tablespoon water

Dice the chicken into small cubes the size of sugar-lumps. In a bowl mix it first with the salt, then the egg white and finally half of the cornflour.

Cut the celery sticks into small chunks diagonally, roughly the same size as the chicken cubes.

Warm the oil in a preheated wok or frying pan and stir-fry the chicken cubes over a moderate heat for 30 seconds or until the flesh has turned white. Lift the chicken from the wok.

Increase the heat and when the oil is very hot, stir-fry the celery for 1 minute. Replace the chicken, add the wine or sherry and soy sauce and cook for a further minute at the most. Combine the remaining cornflour with the water to make a thin paste and add this to the wok, stirring to thicken the sauce. Serve immediately. The chicken should be tender and the celery crisp and crunchy.

■ COOK'S TIP

Since foil is a good conductor of heat it helps to cook the contents of the package quickly, keeping the flavours fresh.

■ COOK'S TIP

Celery is one of the best accompaniments to all kinds of poultry — try this recipe with diced duck breast or turkey, for example. It is very good simply sliced diagonally into very thin strips and stir-fried in hot oil. Cook for 4 minutes, add a good dash of soy sauce and stir until the sauce is absorbed.

93 CHICKEN SALAD

Preparation time: 20-25 minutes	YOU WILL NEED: 450 g/1 lb cooked chicken 1 small cucumber, shredded
Serves 4	50 g/2 oz fresh ginger root, peeled and shredded
Calories: 172 per portion	4 spring onions, white parts only, shredded 1-2 tablespoons freshly chopped parsley, to garnish FOR THE DRESSING 1½ teaspoons salt 1 tablespoon sugar 1 tablespoon lemon juice 1-2 teaspoons chilli sauce 1 tablespoon sesame oil

Make sure the chicken is free of all bones, and remove the skin. Slice the meat into fine shreds the size of a matchstick. Place in a large bowl or deep dish with the shredded cucumber, ginger and spring onions.

Mix together the ingredients for the dressing, adjusting the amount of chilli sauce according to taste. When the dressing is well blended, pour it over the chicken and vegetables and toss well to coat them evenly. Let the salad stand for 1 hour in a cool place before serving, garnished with chopped parsley.

94 CHICKEN AND LEEKS

Preparation time: 5 minutes, plus standing	YOU WILL NEED: ½ cucumber salt 350 g/12 oz boneless chicken breasts, skinned
Cooking time: 2½ minutes	2 tablespoons sunflower oil 3 leeks, thinly sliced diagonally
Serves 4	4 garlic cloves, sliced 1 tablespoon light soy sauce
Calories: 190 per portion	1 tablespoon Chinese wine or dry sherry 1 dried red chilli, crumbled 1 tablespoon freshly chopped coriander coriander leaves, to garnish

Peel the cucumber, cut it in half and remove the seeds. Cut into 2.5 cm/1 inch cubes and place in a colander. Sprinkle with salt and leave to stand for 20 minutes. Cut the chicken into cubes of a similar size.

Heat the oil, add the leeks and garlic and cook for 30 seconds. Add the chicken and brown for 1 minute. Add the soy sauce, wine or sherry and chilli and cook for a further 30 seconds. Stir in the cucumber and cook for 30 seconds. Transfer to a warmed serving dish, sprinkle over the chopped coriander and garnish with coriander leaves. Serve hot.

■ COOK'S TIP

In Chinese cookery presentation is of great importance. Take care when preparing this salad to cut the chicken, cucumber, ginger and spring onions to the same size. Toss the ingredients gently in the dressing so that they are not broken or bruised.

■ COOK'S TIP

Because stir-frying is so rapid a cooking method, it is important to have all the ingredients ready to hand in separate bowls before you begin to cook.

95 STIR-FRIED LEMONY CHICKEN

Preparation time:
5 minutes, plus
marinating

Cooking time:
4 minutes

Serves 4

Calories:
200 per portion

YOU WILL NEED:
350 g/12 oz boneless chicken, skin
    removed
2 tablespoons Chinese wine or
    dry sherry
4 spring onions, chopped
1 x 2.5 cm/1 inch piece fresh root
    ginger, peeled and finely chopped
2 tablespoons sunflower oil
1-2 garlic cloves, sliced
2 celery sticks, sliced diagonally
1 small green pepper, cored, seeded
    and sliced lengthwise
2 tablespoons light soy sauce
juice of ½ lemon
rind of 2 lemons, shredded
¼ teaspoon chilli powder
FOR THE GARNISH
lemon slices
sprig of parsley

Cut the chicken into 7.5 cm/3 inch strips. Mix the wine or
sherry with the spring onions and ginger. Add the chicken and
toss well to coat the pieces. Set aside for 15 minutes.

Heat the oil in a wok or frying pan and add the garlic,
celery and green pepper. Stir-fry for 1 minute. Add the
chicken in its marinade and cook for a further 2 minutes. Stir
in the soy sauce, lemon juice and rind and the chilli powder
and cook for 1 minute more. Transfer to a warmed serving
dish and garnish with lemon slices and a sprig of fresh parsley.

■ COOK'S TIP

To chop root ginger, first
trim the peeled root to a
cube. Cut slices first one way,
keeping the cube together,
then at right angles to give
thin strips to be diced.

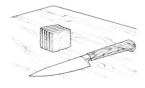

96 CANTONESE CHICKEN, HAM AND GREENS

Preparation time:
25-30 minutes

Cooking time:
about 1½ hours

Serves 4

Calories:
515 per portion

YOU WILL NEED:
1 x 1¼ kg/2½ -2¾ lb chicken
2 slices fresh root ginger, peeled
2 spring onions
2 teaspoons salt
3 tablespoons sunflower oil
225 g/8 oz broccoli or lettuce hearts
225 g/8 oz cooked ham
1 tablespoon cornflour
50 ml/2 fl oz Chinese stock (see
    recipe 2) or cooking liquor

Clean the chicken, place in a saucepan and cover with cold
water. Add the ginger, spring onions and 1½ teaspoons of the
salt. Bring to the boil, cover and simmer gently for 25-30
minutes. Turn off the heat but keep the pan covered and leave
the bird to cook in the hot water for at least 1 hour.

Heat 2 tablespoons of the oil in a wok and stir-fry the
broccoli or lettuce with a little salt. Drain and arrange around
the edge of a serving dish.

Lift the chicken from the saucepan and gently pull the
meat off the bone (with the skin on). Cut into small slices. Cut
the ham into thin slices of the same size. Arrange the chicken
and ham in alternate layers in the middle of the serving dish.

To make a sauce, heat the remaining oil in a clean wok.
Combine the cornflour with the stock to make a paste and
add to the wok. Add the remaining salt and stir over a
moderate heat until thickened. Pour over the meat to glaze.

■ COOK'S TIP

This dish can be served cold
as a starter or part of a
buffet-type meal, or served
hot as a main course for a
splendid dinner. With rice
or noodles it is ample for

4-6 people. To make turnip
flowers for a garnish, use
young tender turnips and
follow the instructions in the
Cook's Tip for recipe 144.

97 CHICKEN CHOP SUEY

Preparation time: 8 minutes	**YOU WILL NEED:** 175 g/6 oz boneless chicken breast, skin removed
Cooking time: 8 minutes	2 tablespoons sunflower oil 5 spring onions, chopped 1 x 2.5 cm/1 inch piece fresh root ginger, peeled and chopped
Serves 4	2 garlic cloves, crushed 1 tablespoon tomato purée
Calories: 230 per portion	2 tablespoons Chinese wine or dry sherry 2 tablespoons light soy sauce 1 teaspoon sugar 8 tablespoons water 275 g/10 oz beansprouts 3 eggs, beaten with 2 tablespoons water

Cut the chicken breast into thin strips. Heat 1 tablespoon of the oil in a wok or frying pan and stir-fry the spring onions and ginger for 1 minute. Add the garlic and chicken strips and stir-fry for 2 minutes. Reduce the heat, add the tomato purée, wine, soy sauce, sugar and 5 tablespoons of the water. Heat through gently, then transfer to a warmed serving dish.

Heat 2 teaspoons of the oil in the wok, add the beansprouts and remaining water and stir-fry for 3 minutes. Add to the serving dish and keep warm.

Wipe the wok clean and heat the remaining oil over a moderate heat. Pour in the beaten eggs and cook until the omelette is set and crisp. Place on top of the chicken and beansprouts and serve at once.

■ COOK'S TIP

Whether serving an omelette as a course on its own or, Chinese style, to be shared among a number of people, prepare it at the last minute and serve immediately before the texture hardens. Because eggs cook in so little heat, it is a good idea to slightly undercook the omelette so that by the time it is served the consistency is perfect.

98 CHICKEN WINGS WITH OYSTER SAUCE

Preparation time: 10 minutes, plus marinating	**YOU WILL NEED:** 450 g/1 lb chicken wings 2 tablespoons sunflower oil 2 leeks, sliced
Cooking time: about 20 minutes	3 tablespoons oyster sauce FOR THE MARINADE 4 spring onions, chopped
Serves 4-6	1 x 1 cm/ ½ inch piece fresh root ginger, peeled and shredded
Calories: 200-140 per portion	1 garlic clove, sliced 1 tablespoon light soy sauce 2 tablespoons Chinese wine or dry sherry FOR THE GARNISH radish waterlilies (see Cook's Tip) cucumber slices

Trim the tips off the chicken wings, then cut them in half at the joints.

To make the marinade, mix the spring onions with the ginger, garlic, soy sauce and wine or sherry. Add the chicken wings, stir well and leave to marinate for 15 minutes.

Heat the oil in a wok or frying pan, add the chicken and marinade and stir-fry for 15 minutes. Add the leeks and oyster sauce and cook for a further 3-4 minutes.

Serve at once, garnished with radish waterlilies and cucumber slices, if liked.

■ COOK'S TIP

For radish waterlilies, cut a row of petal shapes around the radish, keeping them joined at the base. Cut a second row above the first. Put in iced water for an hour.

99 SHREDDED CHICKEN BREAST WITH GREEN PEPPERS

Preparation time:
20-25 minutes

Cooking time:
5 minutes

Serves 4

Calories:
431 per portion

YOU WILL NEED:
2 boneless fresh chicken breasts, skin removed
1½ teaspoons salt
1 egg white, lightly beaten
3 teaspoons cornflour
225 g/8 oz green peppers, seeded
4 tablespoons sunflower oil
1 spring onion, finely chopped
2 slices fresh root ginger, peeled and finely chopped
2 tablespoons Chinese wine
1 teaspoon water
1 teaspoon sesame oil

Cut the chicken into shreds. Mix the meat first with ½ teaspoon of the salt, then the egg white and finally 2 teaspoons of the cornflour. Shred the green pepper to the same size as the chicken.

Heat the oil in a preheated wok or frying pan over a moderate heat and stir-fry the chicken until the flesh turns white. Remove the chicken from the wok and keep warm.

Increase the heat to high. When the oil is very hot, put in the spring onion and ginger to flavour the oil. Add the green peppers, stir continuously for 30 seconds, then return the chicken to the wok with the remaining salt and the wine. Stir for 30 seconds or so, then add the remaining cornflour, mixed with the water. Blend well, and sprinkle over the sesame oil.

■ COOK'S TIP

Marinating with salt, egg white and cornflour before cooking is known as 'velveting' in English cookery. The coating forms an impenetrable barrier *between the meat and the hot oil, preserving the naturally delicate texture of the chicken breast. Chicken that has been deep-frozen is not suitable for this recipe.*

100 PEPPERED SMOKED CHICKEN

Preparation time:
15 minutes

Cooking time:
about 1½ hours

Serves 4

Calories:
476 per portion

YOU WILL NEED:
2 tablespoons Szechuan or black peppercorns
1 tablespoon salt
1 x 1.5 kg/3½ lb roasting chicken
2 tablespoons sesame oil
FUEL FOR SMOKING
3 tablespoons dark brown sugar
2 tablespoons Chinese tea leaves
1 teaspoon ground ginger

Cook the peppercorns in a dry frying pan over a moderate heat for 3 minutes. Crush them coarsely in a pestle and mortar and mix with the salt. Rub this mixture into the chicken skin and inside the body cavity.

Place the chicken in a steamer over gently boiling water. Cover and steam for 1 hour. Lift out the chicken and let it cool.

Line a large, heavy, flameproof lidded casserole with kitchen foil. Mix together the sugar, tea leaves and ginger and place in the casserole. Set a wire rack inside and put the chicken on it. Bring the sides of the foil over the chicken and seal the foil. Put on the lid.

Set the casserole on a moderate heat for 15 minutes. Turn off the heat and leave the chicken standing for 5 minutes. Remove the chicken from the foil and cut it into joints. Arrange on a warmed serving dish and brush with the sesame oil before serving.

■ COOK'S TIP

Once a method of preserving, smoking is now valued for the interesting subtle flavour it imparts to food. Smoking is suitable for all meats and any oily fish.

101 CHICKEN BREAST AND EGG WHITE

Preparation time:
10-15 minutes

Cooking time:
5 minutes

Serves 4

Calories:
274 per portion

YOU WILL NEED:
2 boneless chicken breasts,
    skin removed
1½ teaspoons salt
2 egg whites, lightly beaten
1 tablespoon cornflour
4 tablespoons sunflower oil
1 lettuce heart, separated into leaves
1 slice fresh root ginger, peeled
    and finely chopped
1 spring onion, finely chopped
100 g/4 oz green peas
1 tablespoon Chinese wine or
    dry sherry
1 teaspoon sesame oil

Cut the chicken into small thin slices. Mix them first with ½ teaspoon of the salt, then the egg white, then the cornflour.

Heat the oil in a preheated wok or frying pan over a moderate heat and stir-fry the chicken slices for about 30 seconds or until the flesh turns white. Remove with a slotted spoon.

Increase the heat. Add the lettuce leaves to the hot oil and stir-fry with another ½ teaspoon of the salt until limp. Remove with a slotted spoon and use to line a serving dish.

Add the ginger and spring onion to the wok, then the sliced chicken and peas. Stir in the remaining salt, wine or sherry and stir-fry for 1 minute, blending well. Sprinkle over the sesame oil and transfer to the serving dish. Serve hot.

■ COOK'S TIP

To separate the egg white from the yolk, crack the shell in two over a bowl. Catch the yolk in one half of the shell and let the white fall into the bowl.

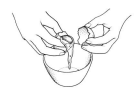

102 DEEP-FRIED DRUMSTICKS

Preparation time:
10 minutes, plus
marinating

Cooking time:
12-15 minutes

Serves 4

Calories:
380 per portion

YOU WILL NEED:
2 tablespoons Chinese wine or
    dry sherry
2 tablespoons light soy sauce
pinch of sugar
4 garlic cloves, crushed
2 teaspoons finely chopped fresh
    root ginger
4 spring onions, chopped
8 chicken drumsticks
50 g/2 oz plain flour
2 small eggs, beaten
sunflower oil for deep-frying
FOR THE GARNISH
lemon slices
parsley sprigs

Place the wine or sherry, soy sauce, sugar, garlic, ginger and spring onions in a bowl. Add the chicken, turn to coat thoroughly and leave to marinate for 30 minutes. Remove the chicken, reserving the marinade.

Sift the flour into a bowl and beat in the eggs. Gradually beat in the marinade to form a smooth batter. Dip the chicken into the batter and turn to coat evenly.

Heat the oil in a wok to 180 C/350 F or until a cube of day-old bread browns in 30 seconds. Deep-fry the chicken for 12-15 minutes until golden and cooked through. Drain on absorbent kitchen paper and serve garnished with lemon slices and sprigs of parsley.

■ COOK'S TIP

These deep-fried drumsticks make an excellent starter or feature in a buffet. The secret is in the savoury batter, which could be varied by the addition of freshly chopped herbs or a teaspoon of sesame seeds. Serve an accompanying dip (see Cook's Tip 19) or satay sauce (Cook's Tip 74) if you wish.

POULTRY & GAME

103 SWEET AND SOUR TURKEY

Preparation time:
6 minutes

Cooking time:
6 minutes

Serves 4

Calories:
120 per portion

YOU WILL NEED:
1 tablespoon sunflower oil
1 onion, finely chopped
1 turkey breast, skinned and cut into
    cubes
½ yellow or red pepper, cored, seeded
    and sliced
3 mushrooms, sliced
spring onion tassel, to garnish
FOR THE SAUCE
1½ tablespoons light soy sauce
1 heaped tablespoon tomato purée
2 teaspoons cornflour
300 ml/ ½ pint water
3 tablespoons unsweetened pineapple
    juice
2 tablespoons wine vinegar
1 heaped teaspoon brown sugar

To make the sauce, place all the ingredients in a small pan and mix well. Bring to the boil, then simmer, stirring until thickened. Keep warm.

Heat the oil in a wok and stir-fry the onion for 2 minutes. Add the turkey and stir-fry for 2-3 minutes. Add the pepper and mushrooms and cook for 2-3 minutes.

Transfer to a warmed serving dish and pour over the sauce. Garnish with spring onion and serve hot.

■ COOK'S TIP

Serve this stir-fried dish with a bowl of plain boiled rice and vegetables such as Braised aubergines (recipe 185) or Stir-fried garlic spinach (recipe 190).

104 PEKING DUCK

Preparation time:
20 minutes, plus
hanging overnight

Cooking time:
about 1 hour

Oven temperature:
200 C, 400 F, gas 6
Serves 4

Calories:
1200 per portion

YOU WILL NEED:
1 x 1.75 kg/4 lb duck
1 tablespoon sugar
1 teaspoon salt
300 ml/ ½ pint water
3 tablespoons yellow bean sauce
2 tablespoons sugar
1 tablespoon sesame oil
1 recipe Mandarin pancakes (see
    recipe 217)
4 small spring onions, cut into strips
½ cucumber, cut into strips
½ red pepper, cored, seeded and cut
    into strips

Hang the duck up by the neck in a cool room. Leave overnight to air-dry thoroughly.

Dissolve 1 tablespoon sugar and salt in the water and rub over the duck. Leave for several hours to dry. Place on a roasting rack and cook in a preheated oven for 1 hour.

Meanwhile, put the yellow bean sauce, two tablespoons sugar and sesame oil in a pan and heat gently for 2-3 minutes, stirring from time to time. Transfer to a sauce bowl.

Carve the duck into neat slices and arrange on a serving dish. Arrange the pancakes on a platter. Place the spring onion strips, cucumber and red pepper on a small dish. Each guest spreads a pancake with a little sauce, adds onion, cucumber and red pepper, then 1-2 slices of duck. The pancake is then rolled up and eaten with the fingers.

■ COOK'S TIP

Peking Duck, eaten in combination with pancakes, vegetables and sauce, provides the perfect example of a unity of contrasting textures with each mouthful.

105 DICED TURKEY WITH CELERY

Preparation time:
5 minutes, plus
soaking

Cooking time:
3 minutes

Serves 4

Calories:
300 per portion

YOU WILL NEED:
4 dried shiitake mushrooms
350 g/12 oz turkey breast, diced
salt
1 egg white, lightly beaten
1 tablespoon cornflour
4 tablespoons sunflower oil
2 garlic cloves, sliced
2 slices fresh root ginger, peeled
and chopped
2 leeks, sliced diagonally
1 small head celery, sliced diagonally
1 red pepper, cored, seeded and sliced
3 tablespoons light soy sauce
2 tablespoons Chinese wine or
dry sherry
celery leaves, to garnish

Soak the mushrooms in boiling water for 15 minutes. Drain, discard the hard stalks and slice the caps.

Mix the turkey pieces first with the salt, then the egg white and finally the cornflour. Heat the oil in a wok and stir-fry the turkey for 1 minute until golden. Remove with a slotted spoon and set aside.

Increase the heat and add the garlic, ginger, leeks and celery and stir-fry for 1 minute. Return the turkey to the wok with the red pepper and cook for 30 seconds. Stir in the soy sauce and sherry and cook for a further 30 seconds.

Spoon into a warmed serving dish and garnish with celery leaves.

■ COOK'S TIP

Removing the skin from the turkey considerably reduces the calorie content of this dish and ensures that the meat keeps its shape in the brief cooking time.

106 TURKEY PARCELS

Preparation time:
15 minutes, plus
marinating

Cooking time:
5 minutes

Serves 4

Calories:
300 per portion

YOU WILL NEED:
1 tablespoon light soy sauce
1 tablespoon Chinese wine or
dry sherry
1 tablespoon sesame oil
450 g/1 lb turkey breast, cut into
16 pieces
4 spring onions, each cut into 4 pieces
1 x 5 cm/2 inch piece fresh root ginger,
peeled and shredded
½ red pepper, cored, seeded
and shredded
1 celery stick, shredded
4 tablespoons sunflower oil

Combine the soy sauce, wine or sherry and sesame oil in a bowl. Add the turkey pieces and toss well to coat them evenly. Leave to marinate for 15-20 minutes.

Cut out 16 pieces of kitchen foil large enough to enclose the turkey pieces generously. Brush the foil with oil, place a piece of turkey in the centre of each and top with a piece of spring onion, a little ginger, pepper and celery. Fold the foil over to enclose and seal the edges well.

Heat the oil in a wok over a moderate heat, add the foil parcels and fry for 2 minutes on each side. Remove the parcels from the oil and leave to drain for 1 minute.

Reheat the oil to very hot and return the turkey parcels to the wok for 1 minute. Drain again and serve immediately. Each guest unwraps his own parcels with chopsticks.

■ COOK'S TIP

The turkey parcels can also be steamed in their foil packages. Place in a bamboo steamer over boiling water and steam vigorously for 10-12 minutes.

107 NANKING SPICED DUCK

Preparation time:
15 minutes, plus 3
days chilling

Cooking time:
1¼ -1½ hours

Oven temperature:
200 C, 400 F, gas 6
Serves 4-6

Calories:
700-460 per portion

YOU WILL NEED:
100 g/4 oz coarse salt
3 teaspoons Szechuan peppercorns
1 x 2 kg/4½ lb duck
FOR THE GARNISH
chilli flowers (see Cook's Tip)
sliced cucumber

Place the salt and peppercorns in a dry frying pan and cook over a high heat for 10 minutes to brown. Shake the pan constantly to prevent the mixture burning, which would give a bitter taste. Leave to cool slightly, then rub the salt and pepper thoroughly over both the inside and outside of the duck. Wrap lightly in foil and store in the refrigerator for 3 days.

Remove the foil and place the duck on a rack in a roasting pan. Cook in a preheated oven for 1¼-1½ hours until golden. Transfer to a warmed serving dish and garnish with chilli flowers and slices of cucumber.

■ COOK'S TIP

For chilli flowers, insert the point of a knife near the stem and slice through, straight down to the tip. Make a second cut at right angles to the first. Ease out the seeds.

108 SZECHUAN SMOKED DUCK

Preparation time:
15 minutes, plus
drying overnight

Cooking time:
1 hour

Serves 4

Calories:
245 per portion

YOU WILL NEED:
1 x 1.5 kg/3 lb duck
3 tablespoons salt
3 teaspoons Szechuan peppercorns
½ teaspoon dried sage
1½ teaspoon ground ginger
1 teaspoon sugar
1.2 litres/2 pints Chinese stock (see recipe 2)
1 tablespoon 5-spice powder
6 spring onions, roughly chopped
6 slices fresh root ginger, peeled
sunflower oil for deep-frying
fuel for smoking (see Cook's Tip)

Dry the duck with absorbent paper. Mix three-quarters of the salt, half the peppercorns, the sage, ground ginger and sugar. Rub the inside of the duck with this mixture and leave it in a cool, well-ventilated place to dry for 24 hours.

Place the duck in a pan and cover with water. Bring to the boil then discard the liquid. Replace it with the stock, add the remaining salt and peppercorns, 5-spice powder, spring onions and root ginger. Simmer 20 minutes, then drain.

Lay the smoking fuel in an old wok and place a wire rack on top. Heat the wok. When it begins to smoke, place the duck on the rack, cover the wok and smoke for 10 minutes on either side, or until the colour darkens to a golden brown.

Heat the oil in a clean wok until it is smoking hot. Lower the duck into the oil and deep-fry over moderate heat for 10 minutes. Lift the duck out and drain carefully.

■ COOK'S TIP

The fuel for smoking the duck in this recipe is 4 tablespoons damp tea leaves, 2 tablespoons brown sugar, 2 tablespoons 5-spice powder, 6 bay leaves and 1 cup hardwood sawdust. Make sure the sawdust is absolutely dry before use.

109 SOY-BRAISED DUCK

Preparation time:
15 minutes, plus
marinating

Cooking time:
about 1½ hours

Oven temperature:
220 C, 425F, gas 7
then
90 C, 375F, gas 5

Serves 4-6

Calories:
850-590 per portion

YOU WILL NEED:
1 × 1.75 kg/4 lb duck
1 × 5 cm/2 inch piece fresh root ginger,
    finely chopped
1 large onion, finely chopped
1 teaspoon salt
6 tablespoons light soy sauce
3 tablespoons malt vinegar
1 tablespoon sunflower oil
4 spring onions, chopped
150 ml/ ¼ pint chicken stock
1 tablespoon cornflour
2 tablespoons water
1 × 227 g/8 oz can pineapple slices
3 tablespoons Chinese wine or
    dry sherry

Prick the duck skin. Combine the ginger, onion and salt and rub over the inside of the duck. Place the duck in a bowl, add the soy sauce and vinegar and marinate 1 hour, spooning the liquid over the duck at intervals. Transfer duck to a roasting pan and cook at the higher temperature for 30 minutes.

Heat the oil in a wok and stir-fry the spring onions until golden. Pour off any excess oil from the duck, sprinkle with the spring onions, marinade and stock. Cover with foil, reduce the oven temperature and cook for 1 hour.

Cut the duck into 16 pieces and arrange on a warmed dish. Blend the cornflour with the water and pineapple juice. Cook for 2 minutes with the halved pineapple slices and the duck juices. Serve the sauce separately.

■ COOK'S TIP

A fatty meat, duck benefits from the acidity of accompanying fruit. Orange is the classic partner in Western cooking, while pineapple has the same role in the East.

110 BRAISED DUCK

Preparation time:
20 minutes, plus
soaking

Cooking time:
about 2½ hours

Serves 4

Calories:
650 per portion

YOU WILL NEED:
4 dried shiitake mushrooms
1 × 1.75 kg/4 lb duck, cut into
    individual portions
5 tablespoons light soy sauce
4 tablespoons sunflower oil
3 spring onions, chopped
4 slices fresh root ginger, peeled
    and chopped
3 star anise
1 teaspoon black peppercorns
2 teaspoons Chinese wine or dry sherry
100 g/4 oz canned bamboo shoots,
    drained and sliced
2 tablespoons cornflour
2 tablespoons water

Soak the mushrooms in boiling water for 20 minutes. Drain and discard the stems.

Rub the duck with a little soy sauce. Heat the oil in a wok or large frying pan and fry the duck until it is golden all over. Transfer the duck to a saucepan, add the spring onions, ginger, star anise, peppercorns, wine or sherry, remaining soy sauce and enough cold water to cover. Bring slowly to the boil, reduce the heat and simmer for 1½-2 hours. Add the mushrooms and bamboo shoots 20 minutes before the end of the cooking time.

Mix the cornflour with the water and stir this mixture into the pan. Continue to cook until the sauce is thickened. Transfer to a warmed serving dish and serve hot.

■ COOK'S TIP

This dish can be prepared a day in advance. Simmer for 1½ hours only and leave to cool completely. To serve, skim off all excess fat, bring back to the boil and add the mushrooms and bamboo shoots. Simmer for 20 minutes and continue as above.

111 DUCK ON SKEWERS

Preparation time:
20-25 minutes, plus marinating

Cooking time:
8-12 minutes

Serves 4

Calories:
260 per portion

YOU WILL NEED:
4 boneless duck breasts, skin removed
FOR THE MARINADE
2 tablespoons brown sugar
1 teaspoon salt
4 tablespoons light soy sauce
1 tablespoon sesame oil
1 x 1 cm/ ½ inch piece fresh root ginger, peeled and finely chopped
1 teaspoon sesame seeds

Cut the duck breasts into 32 evenly sized pieces. Mix the marinade ingredients in a large bowl and add the duck. Stir, cover and marinate for 3-4 hours in a cool place or overnight in the refrigerator. Spoon the marinade over the duck several times to coat the pieces evenly. Remove the duck with a slotted spoon and thread on to 8 bamboo skewers or 4 large metal skewers.

Place the skewers on the grid of a moderately hot barbecue and cook the small skewers for 8-10 minutes, the larger ones for 10-12 minutes. Turn the skewers several times during cooking and baste with the remaining marinade. Serve the barbecued duck hot or cold, either on or off the skewers.

112 JELLIED DUCKLING

Preparation time:
15 minutes, plus setting

Cooking time:
about 4½ hours

Serves 6-8

Calories:
1,120 per portion

YOU WILL NEED:
1 x 2 kg/4½ lb oven-ready duckling
450 g/1 lb belly pork
225 g/8 oz pork rind
250 ml/8 fl oz light soy sauce
1 tablespoon salt
150 ml/ ¼ pint Chinese wine or dry sherry
3 tablespoons sugar
1 teaspoon 5-spice powder
3 spring onions
4 slices fresh root ginger, peeled
sprigs of parsley, to garnish

Place the duckling in a large pan with the belly pork and the pork rind. Cover with water and bring to the boil. Boil for 2-3 minutes, then pour off the water.

Rinse the duckling, pork and pork skin under cold running water and put them back in the pan. Cover with fresh water. Add the soy sauce, salt, wine or sherry, sugar, 5-spice powder, spring onions and ginger. Cover the pan and bring to the boil. Reduce the heat to low and simmer for about 4 hours.

Lift out the duckling, drain and place on a large plate. Remove the meat from the bones very carefully, leaving the skin on. Arrange the meat in a deep oval dish.

Strain the stock, discarding the pork, rind and flavourings. Strain again through a fine-mesh sieve. Pour over the duck pieces. Place the dish in the refrigerator until the stock sets to a jelly. To serve, invert the jellied duckling on to a platter and garnish with sprigs of parsley.

■ COOK'S TIP

This recipe can also be cooked under a preheated hot grill, using 8 small or 4 large skewers.

■ COOK'S TIP

In this Cantonese recipe, the duck is boiled twice in order to reduce the fat content and make the meat very tender. The enriched cooking liquid sets to a delicious jelly and

makes a beautiful dish for a special party. Serve with both plain rice and a composite rice dish such as Yangchow Fried Rice (recipe 203), with a choice of accompaniments.

113 EIGHT-TREASURE DUCK

Preparation time:	YOU WILL NEED:
35-40 minutes	1 x 2 kg/4½ -4¾ lb oven-ready duckling
	2 tablespoons dark soy sauce
Cooking time:	150 g/5 oz glutinous rice
1¼ hours	200 ml/ ⅓ pint water
	4-5 dried shiitake mushrooms
Oven temperature:	1 tablespoon dried shrimps
200 C, 400 F, gas 6	2 tablespoons sunflower oil
then	2 spring onions, finely chopped
180 C, 350 F, gas 4	2 slices fresh root ginger, chopped
	100 g/4 oz bamboo shoots, cubed
Serves 4-6	100 g/4 oz cooked ham, cubed
	½ teaspoon salt
Calories:	1 tablespoon light soy sauce
1031-688 per portion	2 tablespoons Chinese wine

Brush the duck skin with the soy sauce.

Cook the rice in the water (see recipe 206). Prepare the mushrooms (see recipe 6). Soak the shrimps in warm water for 20 minutes and drain.

Heat the oil in a wok and stir-fry the spring onions and ginger 30 seconds. Add the remaining ingredients, blend well, then turn off the heat, add the cooked rice and mix all the ingredients together.

Pack this mixture into the duck cavity and close up the tail opening. Bake the duck on a wire rack in a pan in a preheated oven at the higher temperature for 30 minutes. Reduce the heat for a further 45 minutes.

Spoon the stuffing out of duck on to the centre of a dish. Cut the duck into neat pieces and arrange round the edge.

■ COOK'S TIP

The name of this dish refers to the various ingredients used for the stuffing. If glutinous rice is unavailable, use round pudding rice instead.

114 HOT AND SPICY QUAIL

Preparation time:	YOU WILL NEED:
20 minutes, plus	4 oven-ready quail
marinating	3 tablespoons sesame oil for grilling
	FOR THE MARINADE
Cooking time:	2 tablespoons sunflower oil
15-20 minutes	3 garlic cloves, crushed
	4 spring onions, finely chopped
Serves 4	1 stem lemon grass, finely chopped
	½ teaspoon cayenne pepper
Calories:	5 drops of Worcestershire sauce
198 per portion	1 tablespoon nam pla (fish sauce)
	1 teaspoon sugar
	⅓ teaspoon salt
	ACCOMPANIMENT
	lemon dip (see recipe 116)

Use a sharp knife to split the quail down the spine. Splay the halves and flatten them with a cleaver.

For the marinade, heat the oil in a pan and add the garlic, spring onions and lemon grass. Cook over moderate heat for 2-3 minutes. Leave to cool. Stir in the cayenne pepper, Worcestershire sauce, nam pla, sugar and salt.

Place the quail in a shallow dish large enough to hold them in a single layer. Pour the marinade over, cover the dish and marinate 2 hours. Turn the quail over from time to time.

Drain the birds and thread on to skewers. Arrange under a preheated moderate grill and brush liberally with sesame oil. Grill for 15-20 minutes or until cooked, turning frequently and brushing with more oil as necessary. Serve immediately with lemon dip.

■ COOK'S TIP

In China, quails are looked upon as symbols of plenty. A brace of these little game birds makes a substantial meal for one person; this recipe for 4 is intended as part of a varied menu. The marinade is important to counteract the meat's tendency to dryness.

115 PLEASURE BOAT DUCK

Preparation time:
30 minutes

Cooking time:
1¼ -1½ hours

Oven temperature:
220 C, 425F, gas 6

Serves 4-6

Calories:
894-596 per portion

YOU WILL NEED:
1 x 1.75 kg/4 lb oven-ready duck
4 dried Chinese mushrooms
2 tablespoons sunflower oil
4 spring onions, chopped
1 x 2.5 cm/1 inch piece fresh root
    ginger, peeled and chopped
100 g/4 oz lean pork, shredded
50 g/2 oz cooked broad beans
FOR THE GLAZE
3 tablespoons light soy sauce
1 tablespoon Chinese wine or
    dry sherry
1 tablespoon sesame oil
FOR THE GARNISH
turnip flowers (see recipe 144)
radishes
mint leaves

Immerse the duck in a pan of boiling water for 2 minutes, then drain well. Soak the mushrooms in boiling water for 15 minutes. Drain, discard the stems and slice the caps.

Heat the oil in a small pan and fry the spring onions, ginger and pork for 2 minutes. Add the beans and cook for 1 minute. Stir in the mushrooms and leave to cool. Use this mixture to stuff the duck, and sew it up securely.

Combine the ingredients for the glaze and brush over the duck. Place in a roasting pan and cook in a preheated oven for 1¼ -1½ hours, basting occasionally. Transfer to a serving plate and garnish as shown. Serve at once.

■ COOK'S TIP

To reduce the fattiness of roast duck, prick the bird all over with a fork and stand it on a wire rack in the roasting pan so that the juices collect beneath it.

116 ROAST PIGEONS

Preparation time:
30 minutes, plus
standing

Cooking time:
20 minutes

Oven temperature:
230 C, 450 F, gas 8

Serves 4

Calories:
470 per portion

YOU WILL NEED:
4 oven-ready pigeons
175 ml/6 fl oz rice alcohol or vodka
FOR THE MARINADE
5 tablespoons sunflower oil
3 garlic cloves, crushed
½ onion, finely chopped
2 tablespoons light soy sauce
2 teaspoons honey or golden syrup
⅓ teaspoon 5-spice powder
pinch of freshly ground black pepper
6 tablespoons water
LEMON DIP
2 lemons, cut in quarters
2 teaspoons salt
freshly ground black pepper

Prepare the pigeons by rubbing them inside and out with rice alcohol or vodka. Place on a wire rack and set aside to dry.

Combine the ingredients for the marinade. Paint the pigeons with this mixture inside and out, and leave for 1 hour to dry, either on a rack in a cool well-ventilated room or preferably hanging by their necks.

Brush the pigeons with the remaining marinade and roast on a rack in a pan for 20 minutes.

Strip the flesh from the cooked pigeons and arrange on a warmed plate. Divide the lemon wedges among 4 dinner plates and add ½ teaspoon salt and a pinch of pepper to each. Guests make their own dip by mixing the salt and pepper and moistening the mixture with a squeeze of lemon juice.

■ COOK'S TIP

Pigeons are not as popular as duck but are still widely used in Chinese cooking, usually braised or deep-fried. This recipe for roast pigeons succeeds because they are *marinated first to tenderize the flesh and keep it from drying out.*

MEAT DISHES

Pork is the most widely used meat in China, partly because there are no religious restrictions on the killing of pigs. Most lamb dishes derive from Chinese Mohammedans. When the sacred ox, symbol of spring, occurs in Chinese food, the results are completely irresistible.

117 CHA SHAO

Preparation time:	YOU WILL NEED:
15 minutes, plus marinating	1 kg/2 lb boned pork shoulder
	FOR THE MARINADE
	2 tablespoons soy sauce
Cooking time:	2 tablespoons Chinese wine or
40-45 minutes	dry sherry
	2 teaspoons sesame oil
Oven temperature:	1 teaspoon salt
180 C, 350 F, gas 4	2 teaspoons ginger juice (see Cook's Tip)
Serves 4	2 tablespoons clear honey or golden syrup
Calories:	50 g/2 oz sugar
263 per portion	1-2 garlic cloves, crushed

Cut the meat into chunks 5 x 5 x 10 cm/2 x 2 x 4 inches in size. Mix the marinade ingredients together in a dish, add the pork and leave to marinate for at least 6 hours in the refrigerator. Turn the pieces occasionally.

Place the pork on a wire rack in a roasting pan. Cook in a preheated oven for 40-45 minutes or until tender, basting frequently with the pan juices.

Cut the pork into smaller pieces for serving and arrange on a plate. Serve hot or cold.

118 OMELETTE WITH MEAT SAUCE

Preparation time:	YOU WILL NEED:
15 minutes	3 tablespoons sunflower oil
	1 garlic clove, crushed
Cooking time:	2 spring onions, chopped
20-25 minutes	2 celery sticks, chopped
	1 boneless chicken breast, diced
Serves 4-6	100 g/4 oz minced pork
	2 teaspoons cornflour
Calories:	1 tablespoon water
360-240 per portion	1 tablespoon Chinese wine or dry sherry
	2 tablespoons light soy sauce
	6 eggs, beaten
	salt and pepper

Heat 1 tablespoon of the oil in a saucepan. Add the garlic, spring onions and celery and cook for 1 minute over moderate heat. Add the chicken and pork and cook, stirring, for 2 minutes. Blend the cornflour with the water and stir this thin paste into the sauce with the wine or sherry and soy sauce. Simmer for 15 minutes.

Meanwhile, make the omelette. Season the eggs with salt and pepper to taste. Heat the remaining oil in a large frying pan over a gentle heat. Add the eggs and cook until the omelette is lightly set and browned on both sides.

Place the omelette on a warmed serving dish and spoon over the meat sauce. Serve at once, with a garnish of spring onions and celery leaves if liked.

▓ COOK'S TIP

To extract ginger juice from the root, place small peeled slices of root ginger in a garlic crusher and squeeze firmly.

▓ COOK'S TIP

With an omelette base, this sauce can be varied according to taste. Diced ham can be substituted for the pork; instead of chicken, partner the pork with shrimps. Add *1 grated carrot for sweetness, with 2-3 tomatoes, skinned and diced, for colour.*

119 STIR-FRIED PORK WITH BAMBOO SHOOT

Preparation time:
5 minutes, plus
marinating

Cooking time:
4 minutes

Serves 4

Calories:
118 per portion

YOU WILL NEED:
225 g/8 oz lean pork fillet, thinly sliced
1 teaspoon Chinese wine or dry sherry
2 tablespoons light soy sauce
3 tablespoons sunflower oil
1 garlic clove, peeled and chopped
275 g/10 oz bamboo shoots,
    thinly sliced
2 teaspoons vinegar
3 spring onions, shredded

Place the pork in a bowl with the wine or sherry and 2 teaspoons of the soy sauce. Mix well, then leave to marinate for 20 minutes or so.

Heat the oil in a wok or frying pan over moderate heat. Add the garlic and fry until golden brown to flavour the oil. Remove the garlic with a slotted spoon and discard.

Add the pork to the wok and stir-fry until it changes colour. Add the bamboo shoot, the remaining soy sauce and the vinegar. Stir-fry for 30 seconds. Add the spring onion and continue to cook for 30 seconds more. Transfer to a warmed dish and serve hot.

120 STIR-FRIED LIVER WITH SPINACH

Preparation time:
10 minutes

Cooking time:
3-4 minutes

Serves 4

Calories:
300 per portion

YOU WILL NEED:
350 g/12 oz pig's liver, cut into thin
    triangular slices
2 tablespoons cornflour
4 tablespoons sunflower oil
450 g/1 lb fresh spinach, washed
    and drained
1 teaspoon salt
2 thin slices fresh root ginger, peeled
1 tablespoon light soy sauce
1 tablespoon Chinese wine or
    dry sherry
shredded spring onion, to garnish

Blanch the slices of liver in boiling water for a few seconds. Drain and coat with cornflour.

Heat 2 tablespoons of the oil in a wok or frying pan. Add the spinach and salt and stir-fry for 2 minutes. Remove from the pan and arrange around the edge of a warmed serving dish. Keep hot.

Wipe the wok clean with absorbent kitchen paper. Heat the remaining oil in the wok until very hot. Add the ginger, liver, soy sauce and wine or sherry. Stir-fry briskly for 1-2 minutes – avoid overcooking or the liver will become tough. Pour the mixture over the spinach and serve at once, garnished with spring onions.

■ COOK'S TIP

Soy sauce is one of the most important ingredients in Chinese cookery, often used in combination with wine, sugar and stock. As it is salty, be careful not to use too *much. Light soy sauce has a more delicate flavour, best for dips and quickly cooked dishes. Dark soy sauce is suitable only for long stewing.*

■ COOK'S TIP

Blanching liver in boiling water is a useful way of ensuring that it remains tender during the cooking process. Serve this dish with plain boiled noodles.

121 BEEF WITH PLUMS

Preparation time:	YOU WILL NEED:
6 minutes	1 tablespoon sunflower oil
	1 onion, thinly sliced
Cooking time:	1 garlic clove, crushed
8 minutes	350 g/12 oz lean beef, cut into
	thin slivers
Serves 4	2-3 dessert plums, stoned and cut
	into slices
Calories:	3 flat mushrooms, sliced
220 per portion	1 tablespoon Chinese wine or
	dry sherry
	2 teaspoons soft brown sugar
	1 tablespoon dark soy sauce
	2 teaspoons cornflour
	2 tablespoons water
	chopped spring onions (green part
	only), to garnish

Heat the oil in a large frying pan, add the onion and fry for 2 minutes. Stir in the garlic and beef and stir-fry over a high heat for 2 minutes. Reduce the heat and add the plums and mushrooms. Continue to stir-fry for 1 minute, then stir in the wine or sherry, sugar and soy sauce. Blend the cornflour with the water to make a thin paste and add this mixture to the pan, stirring until the sauce has thickened. Transfer to a warmed dish and serve at once, garnished with chopped spring onion.

122 SWEET AND SOUR BEEF STEW

Preparation time:	YOU WILL NEED:
20 minutes	1 kg/2 lb lean stewing beef, cut into
	5 cm/2 inch cubes
Cooking time:	1 large onion, thinly sliced
about 1¼ hours	4 fresh green chillies, seeded and
	thinly sliced
Serves 4-6	2 thin slices fresh root ginger, crushed
	2 large garlic cloves, crushed
Calories:	2 tablespoons sunflower oil
500-360 per portion	1 teaspoon laos powder (see recipe 88)
	475 ml/16 fl oz beef stock
	2 tablespoons honey
	4 tablespoons red wine vinegar
	2 teaspoons Worcestershire sauce
	salt

Combine the beef, onion, chillies, ginger, garlic, oil and laos powder in a large pan. Place over moderately high heat and cook for 5-10 minutes, stirring occasionally, until the meat has browned on all sides.

Stir in the remaining ingredients and bring to the boil, stirring frequently. Reduce the heat and simmer for 1 hour or until the sauce is reduced to a thick glaze.

Transfer the stew to a heated serving dish and serve with boiled rice.

COOK'S TIP

Plums add a delicious sweetness to beef dishes and a contrast of texture. Depending on the ripeness of the fruit you may need to amend the amount of sugar..

COOK'S TIP

This stew has a robust flavour that needs the accompaniment of plain boiled rice but sharp-flavoured vegetables. Serve with Crunchy pickled cucumber (recipe 222) and Mustard-pickled aubergine (recipe 223) or Stir-fried garlic spinach (recipe 190).

123 KOREAN SPICED RAW BEEF

Preparation time:
20-30 minutes

Serves 4

Calories:
420 per portion (340 per portion without egg yolks)

YOU WILL NEED:
450 g/1 lb lean steak (fillet or rump, for example)
2 teaspoons sugar
2 teaspoons sesame seeds
1 tablespoon sesame oil
1 tablespoon crushed garlic
salt
4 egg yolks (optional)
FOR THE GARNISH
2 small pears, peeled and cut into strips
12 diagonal slices of cucumber, cut into strips
parsley sprigs
carrot flowers (see Cook's Tip)

Cut the meat into very thin slices no more than 3 mm/⅛ inch thick. Cut the slices into matchstick strips. Place in a bowl with the sugar, sesame seeds, sesame oil, garlic and salt. Mix together thoroughly and divide into 4 equal portions.

Divide the pear and cucumber strips equally between 4 serving plates, arranging them in separate piles. Place the meat mixture on top. If using egg yolks, shape the mixture into a neat mound with a hollow on top and place an egg yolk in each hollow. Garnish with sprigs of parsley and carrot flowers and serve immediately.

124 FRIED BEEF WITH SCRAMBLED EGG

Preparation time:
15 minutes

Cooking time:
5-10 minutes

Serves 4

Calories:
450 per portion

YOU WILL NEED:
½ teaspoon freshly grated root ginger
1 tablespoon Chinese wine or dry sherry
1 teaspoon sugar
2 teaspoons light soy sauce
1 tablespoon cornflour
5 tablespoons sunflower oil
225 g/8 oz lean beef, thinly sliced across the grain
4 large eggs
salt and pepper
oil for deep frying
1 spring onion, chopped

Mix the ginger with the wine or sherry, sugar, soy sauce, cornflour and 1 tablespoon of the oil. Cut the slices of beef into bite-sized pieces and toss them in this mixture. Leave to marinate while preparing the eggs.

Beat the eggs with 1 tablespoon of the oil and salt and pepper to taste until light and fluffy.

Deep-fry the beef over a moderate heat for a few seconds, until it changes colour. Lift out of the oil and drain on absorbent kitchen paper.

Heat the remaining 3 tablespoons of oil in a pan over a high heat. Add the deep-fried beef and eggs and stir-fry briskly for 30 seconds. Add the spring onions and stir-fry until the eggs are cooked. Serve at once.

▨ COOK'S TIP

To make carrot flowers, trim the ends of young carrots and make 'V' cuts evenly along the length with a sharp knife. Cut across into thin slices of equal thickness.

▨ COOK'S TIP

If your menu includes a dish such as this, which needs last-minute attention, include other recipes such as steamed or braised fish or meat or composite rice dishes which can stand for a few minutes without spoiling.

125 PEKING NOODLES

Preparation time:
10 minutes

Cooking time:
6 minutes

Serves 4-6

Calories:
600-410 per portion

YOU WILL NEED:
450 g/1 lb fresh wholewheat noodles
1 tablespoon sunflower oil
1 onion, thinly sliced
1 x 2.5 cm/1 inch piece fresh root
    ginger, chopped
1 garlic clove, crushed
225 g/8 oz lean minced beef
1 tablespoon light soy sauce
2 tablespoons Chinese wine or
    dry sherry
2-3 teaspoons sugar
1 tablespoon cornflour
4 tablespoons water

Cook the noodles in a large pan of boiling salted water for about 3 minutes. Drain and keep warm.

Heat the oil in a large frying pan and stir-fry the onion, ginger and garlic for 1½ minutes. Add the beef and stir-fry until it is evenly browned. Stir in the soy sauce, wine or sherry and sugar and continue to stir-fry for 2 minutes. Mix the cornflour with the water to make a thin paste and add this to the pan, stirring until the sauce is thickened.

Divide the noodles between warmed individual plates and spoon the meat sauce over them. Serve at once.

126 OXTAIL NOODLES

Preparation time:
15 minutes

Cooking time:
about 4 hours

Oven temperature:
180 C, 350 F, gas 4

Serves 6

Calories:
1,009 per portion

YOU WILL NEED:
1.75 kg/4 lb, oxtail, cut up
450 g/1 lb rice stick noodles
600 ml/ 1 pint beef stock
1 chicken stock cube
4 tablespoons dark soy sauce
freshly ground black pepper
3 tablespoons hoisin sauce
2 tablespoons yellow bean paste
1 tablespoon sugar
6 tablespoons Chinese wine or
    dry sherry
5 spring onions, finely chopped
1½ tablespoons cornflour
5 tablespoons water

Parboil the oxtail in boiling water for 5-6 minutes and drain. Cook the noodles in boiling water for 5 minutes, then drain.

Heat the stock in a flameproof casserole. Add the crumbled stock cube, soy sauce, pepper, hoisin sauce, yellow bean paste, sugar and half the wine. Bring to the boil and add the oxtail. Cover and cook in a preheated oven for 3½ hours, stirring every 30 minutes and adding water if necessary.

Place the noodles in a wok. Sprinkle with the spring onion and spoon over the gravy from the casserole. Stir over a moderate heat for 3 minutes. Transfer to a large dish.

Sprinkle the remaining wine over the oxtail in the casserole. Blend the cornflour and water and pour over the meat. Stir over a moderate heat to coat the meat with sauce. Arrange the meat and sauce on top of the noodles. Serve hot.

▨ COOK'S TIP

It is not difficult to see the similarity between dishes such as this and Italian pasta dishes with a sauce — in fact Marco Polo is credited with having brought the idea home with him after his travels in the East. Serve with a selection of fresh, raw vegetables such as red, yellow and green peppers, cucumber and celery, all cut into strips.

▨ COOK'S TIP

This Szechuan dish is full of flavour, and makes a perfect winter meal. Serve with a green vegetable such as Hot and sour cabbage (recipe 174).

127 DEEP-FRIED BEEF SLICES

Preparation time:
10 minutes, plus
marinating

Cooking time:
3-5 minutes

Serves 4-6

Calories:
380-250 per portion

YOU WILL NEED:
4 *spring onions, chopped*
pinch of salt
1 *tablespoon Chinese wine or*
 dry sherry
1 x 2.5 *cm/1 inch piece fresh root*
 ginger, chopped
1 *tablespoon chilli sauce*
1 *fresh chilli, seeded and chopped*
450 *g/1 lb rump steak, thinly sliced*
oil for deep-frying
FOR THE BATTER
4 *tablespoons plain flour*
pinch of salt
1 *egg*
3-4 *tablespoons water*
FOR THE GARNISH
lemon quarters
coriander leaves

Combine the spring onions, salt, wine or sherry, ginger, chilli
sauce and chopped chilli in a bowl and add the sliced steak.
Toss well to coat and leave to marinate for 20-25 minutes.

To make the batter, sift the flour and salt into a bowl and
make a well in the centre. Break in the egg and beat well,
adding sufficient water to give a smooth consistency.

Heat the oil in a wok or deep-frier. Dip the steak slices into
the batter and deep-fry until golden. Drain on absorbent
kitchen paper and serve at once, garnished with lemon
quarters and coriander leaves.

128 SZECHUAN HOT SHREDDED BEEF

Preparation time:
10-15 minutes

Cooking time:
about 10 minutes

Serves 4-6

Calories:
400-270 per portion

YOU WILL NEED:
450 *g/1 lb rump or frying steak*
2 *tablespoons cornflour*
salt
3 *tablespoons sunflower oil*
4 *spring onions, chopped*
2 *celery sticks, sliced diagonally*
4 *carrots, sliced diagonally*
2 *tablespoons light soy sauce*
1 *tablespoon hoisin sauce*
3 *teaspoons chilli sauce*
2 *tablespoons Chinese wine or*
 dry sherry

Cut the steak into long thin slices 5 cm/2 inches thick. Toss
the steak in the cornflour and season with salt to taste.

Heat the oil in a wok or frying pan over a moderate heat.
Add the spring onions and stir-fry for 1 minute. Add the sliced
steak and cook for 4 minutes, stirring, until the meat is lightly
browned. Add the celery and carrots and cook for 2 minutes.
Stir in the soy, hoisin and chilli sauces and the wine or sherry,
bring to the boil and cook for 1 minute.

Arrange on a warmed serving dish and serve at once.

▒ COOK'S TIP

*Deep-fried in batter, this is a
rich meat dish which benefits
from a sharp, fresh
accompaniment, such as
Festive vegetable achar
(recipe 221) or simply a*

*platter of mixed raw
vegetables with lemon juice
and soy sauce for dipping.*

▒ COOK'S TIP

*To use a less expensive cut of
beef, marinate it first in a
little Chinese wine, soy sauce
and sesame oil in order to
soften it and keep it moist.*

129 STIR-FRIED ORANGE BEEF

Preparation time:
5 minutes, plus
marinating

Cooking time:
7 minutes

Serves 4

Calories:
370 per portion

YOU WILL NEED:
350 g/12 oz rump steak
2 teaspoons sesame oil
2 tablespoons dark soy sauce
1 tablespoon Chinese wine or
    dry sherry
1 x 2.5 cm/1 inch piece fresh root
    ginger, finely chopped
2 teaspoons cornflour
4 tablespoons sunflower oil
2 dried red chillies,crumbled
shredded rind of 1 orange
pinch of salt
½ teaspoon roasted Szechuan
    peppercorns, finely ground
1 teaspoon light soft brown sugar
orange slices, to garnish

Cut the beef into thin slices 5 cm/2 inches long, cutting against the grain.

Combine 1 teaspoon of sesame oil, 1 tablespoon of soy sauce, the wine or sherry, ginger and cornflour. Add the beef and toss to coat well. Let marinate 15 minutes, then drain.

Heat the oil in a wok and quickly brown the meat. Remove from the wok and drain on absorbent paper. Pour off all but 1 tablespoon of oil from the wok. Heat the oil until it is very hot, add the chillies and stir-fry for 30 seconds. Return the beef to the wok and add the orange rind, salt, pepper, sugar and remaining soy sauce. Stir-fry for 4 minutes, sprinkle with remaining sesame oil and serve, garnished with orange slices.

130 BEEF WITH HOT SALAD

Preparation time:
10 minutes

Cooking time:
5-8 minutes

Serves 4

Calories:
250 per portion

YOU WILL NEED:
450 g/1 lb fillet steak
1 large onion, sliced into rings
2 fresh chillies (green or red)
2 garlic cloves, crushed
½ teaspoon sugar
½ teaspoon light soy sauce
juice of 1 lime or 1 lemon
1 teaspoon freshly chopped mint
selection of fresh vegetables, to serve
    (see Cook's Tip)

Cut the beef along the grain into 2.5 cm/1 inch strips about 6 cm/2½ inches long and 1 cm/ ½ inch thick. Put the onion rings and chillies on a skewer and grill under a preheated moderate grill until soft. Remove them from the skewer and mash together.

Grill the beef until it is cooked to taste; do not overcook. Mix the beef slices with the mashed onion and chilli, then add the garlic, sugar, soy sauce, lime or lemon juice and the chopped mint. Place on a warmed serving plate and serve surrounded with a selection of fresh seasonal vegetables.

▓ COOK'S TIP

Orange makes an excellent accompaniment to beef. The perfect vegetable to serve with this delicious dish is Stir-fried garlic spinach (recipe 190), with boiled noodles.

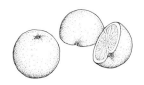

▓ COOK'S TIP

As well as the tomatoes, cucumbers and Chinese cabbage shown with this dish, try celery, chicory, watercress, beansprouts and red, yellow or orange

peppers. Cut into strips or arrange in bunches according to type as a border to the meat.

131 STEWED BEEF WITH CARROTS

Preparation time:
15 minutes

Cooking time:
about 2 hours

Serves 4

Calories:
435 per portion

YOU WILL NEED:
750 g/1½ lb stewing steak, trimmed
    of fat
2 tablespoons sunflower oil
1 x 2.5 cm/1 inch piece fresh root
    ginger, peeled and finely chopped
1 spring onion, chopped
1 garlic clove, crushed
4 tablespoons light soy sauce
1 tablespoon Chinese wine or
    dry sherry
1 tablespoon sugar
½ tablespoon 5-spice powder
450 g/1 lb carrots, peeled

Cut the meat into 1 cm/ ½ inch cubes.

Heat the oil in a heavy saucepan or flameproof casserole. Add the ginger, spring onion and garlic, stirring well to mix. Stir-fry gently for 2 minutes to flavour the oil.

Add the beef and the soy sauce, wine or sherry, sugar and 5-spice powder. Toss gently to mix then pour in just enough cold water to cover. Bring to the boil, then reduce the heat, cover the pan and simmer for 1½ hours. Stir occasionally to ensure that the beef cooks evenly.

Cut the carrots diagonally into diamond shapes. Add to the beef and simmer for a further 30 minutes, or until both beef and carrots are tender. Transfer to a warmed serving dish and serve hot.

132 STIR-FRIED CHILLI BEEF

Preparation time:
20 minutes

Cooking time:
3½ minutes

Serves 4

Calories:
340 per portion

YOU WILL NEED:
450 g/1 lb rump steak
salt
2 tablespoons sunflower oil
2 dried red chillies
2 garlic cloves, sliced
1 x 2.5 cm/1 inch piece fresh root
    ginger, shredded
4 spring onions, shredded
2 tablespoons dark soy sauce
2 tablespoons light soy sauce
2 tablespoons Chinese wine or
    dry sherry
2 fresh green chillies, seeded
    and chopped

Cut the steak into thin slices across the grain, and season well with salt.

Heat the oil in a wok or deep frying pan over a moderate heat and fry the red chillies for 1 minute to flavour the oil. Remove from the wok with a slotted spoon and discard. Increase the heat, add the steak and stir-fry for 1 minute, until browned. Add the garlic, ginger and spring onions and cook for 30 seconds. Pour over the soy sauces and wine or sherry, add the chopped green chillies and cook for a further minute. Transfer to a warmed serving dish and serve at once.

■ COOK'S TIP

As with many stews, this one tastes even better if made a day in advance. This will also give you the opportunity to remove any excess fat once the sauce has cooled. Keep

chilled then bring back to the boil before serving.

■ COOK'S TIP

Because stir-frying is so rapid, the cooking oil is often flavoured first, either with chillies, as here, or with garlic or ginger. The flavouring agent is usually discarded.

133 RAPID-FRIED LAMB SLICES

Preparation time:
15-20 minutes, plus
marinating

Cooking time:
2 minutes

Serves 4

Calories:
284 per portion

YOU WILL NEED:
225-275 g/8-10 oz leg of lamb fillet,
    all fat removed
approx 12 spring onions
4 tablespoons sunflower oil
1 tablespoon light soy sauce
½ teaspoon salt
1 tablespoon Chinese wine or
    dry sherry
½ teaspoon freshly ground Szechuan
    or black pepper
2 teaspoons cornflour
1 garlic clove, crushed
1 tablespoon sesame oil
1 tablespoon wine vinegar

Slice the lamb fillet as thinly as possible. Cut the spring onions
in half lengthways, then slice them diagonally into 5 cm/2 inch
lengths.

Place the meat and spring onions in a shallow dish and add
1 tablespoon sunflower oil, the soy sauce, salt, wine or sherry,
pepper and cornflour. Turn to coat the meat evenly and leave
to marinate for 30 minutes.

Heat the remaining sunflower oil in a wok until it is very
hot. Add the crushed garlic to flavour the oil, then add the
lamb and spring onions in the marinade. Stir-fry over a high
heat for 30 seconds. Sprinkle over the sesame oil and vinegar,
stir briefly and serve immediately.

134 TUNG-PO LAMB

Preparation time:
15 minutes

Cooking time:
20-25 minutes

Serves 4-6

Calories:
370-250 per portion

YOU WILL NEED:
2 tablespoons sunflower oil
675 g/1½ lb very lean lamb, thinly
    sliced
225 g/8 oz carrots, sliced diagonally
4 celery sticks, sliced diagonally
3 tablespoons light soy sauce
4 tablespoons Chinese wine or
    dry sherry
2 leeks, sliced
4 garlic cloves, thinly sliced
4 spring onions, cut into 2.5 cm/1 inch
    lengths
1 x 5 cm/2 inch piece fresh root ginger,
    peeled and shredded
1 teaspoon lightly crushed black
    peppercorns
2 teaspoons sugar

Heat the oil in a wok or deep frying pan, add the lamb and
brown on all sides. Reduce the heat, add the carrots and
celery and stir-fry for 2 minutes. Stir in the soy sauce and wine
or sherry. Cover and cook for 15 minutes, until the vegetables
are tender.

Add the leeks, garlic, spring onions and ginger and cook
for 1 minute. Add the peppercorns and sugar and heat
through, stirring, until the sugar dissolves. Serve at once.

COOK'S TIP

*In order for the meat to be
tender and juicy, it is
essential to cook this recipe
over the highest heat in the
shortest possible time. Heat
the wok for a few minutes*
*before adding the oil.
Because the meat is very
thinly sliced it will cook
through almost at once.*

COOK'S TIP

*The ideal cut for this dish is
lean, boneless leg of lamb,
from which all visible fat has
been removed. You could
also use trimmed best end of
neck cutlets.*

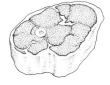

135 MONGOLIAN LAMB HOT POT

Preparation time:
20 minutes

Cooking time:
about 20-30 minutes
(see method)

Serves 4-6

Calories:
430-290 per portion

YOU WILL NEED:
1 kg/2 lb lamb fillet, frozen
50 g/2 oz cellophane noodles
1 large Chinese cabbage, finely
    shredded
450 g/1 lb young spinach, finely
    shredded
2 cakes bean curd, thinly sliced
2.25 litres/4 pints Chinese stock (see
    recipe 2)

Cut the lamb while it is partially frozen into paper-thin slices and arrange neatly on a serving dish; leave to thaw.

Soak the noodles in hot water for 10 minutes; drain. Place the cabbage leaves and the spinach in a dish and arrange the slices of bean curd and the noodles on another dish.

Heat the stock in a fondue pot or similar vessel at the table. Using bamboo chopsticks, each diner then dips a slice of the meat into the hot stock to cook it, then dips the meat into a sauce (see Cook's Tip), and eats it with the noodles, green leaves and bean curd. When all of the meat has been eaten, the remaining vegetables, bean curd and noodles are added to the pot and cooked for about 5-10 minutes. This soup is eaten at the end of the meal.

136 SPICED LEG OF LAMB

Preparation time:
15 minutes, plus
marinating

Cooking time:
2½ hours

Oven temperature:
180 C, 350 F, gas 4

Serves 4

Calories:
530 per portion

YOU WILL NEED:
1.75-2.5 kg/4-5 lb leg of lamb
6 garlic cloves, crushed
6 slices fresh root ginger, peeled
    and shredded
2 onions, thinly sliced
1.2 litres/2 pints Chinese stock (see
    recipe 2)
5 tablespoons light soy sauce
3 tablespoons soy bean paste or
    hoisin sauce
2 tablespoons dried chilli pepper or
    chilli sauce
½ teaspoon 5-spice powder
2 tablespoons sugar
300 ml/ ½ pint red wine
1 chicken stock cube

Place all the ingredients except the lamb in a saucepan and simmer gently for 45 minutes.

Place the lamb in another pan, pour over the sauce and bring to the boil. Simmer gently for 1½ hours, turning the lamb every 30 minutes. Remove the pan from the heat and leave the lamb to cool in the sauce. Leave in a cool place to marinate for 3 hours or overnight.

About 1 hour before serving, remove the lamb from the sauce, place in a roasting pan and cook in a preheated oven for 1 hour. To serve, slice the lamb into bite-sized pieces. Serve hot or cold.

◾ COOK'S TIP

This dish is served with several sauces. In one bowl put 6 chopped spring onions and 2 tablespoons shredded fresh root ginger; in another 6 tablespoons sesame seed paste (tahini) mixed with 3 tablespoons sesame oil. Put light soy sauce, chilli sauce and freshly chopped coriander leaves in individual bowls.

◾ COOK'S TIP

Serve this dish hot or cold with dips such as hoisin sauce, soy sauce and Chinese wine or dry sherry mixed together, or soy sauce mixed with a little vinegar.

137 JELLIED LAMB

Preparation time:
25-30 minutes, plus setting

Cooking time:
2½ hours

Serves 6

Calories:
224 per portion

YOU WILL NEED:
675 g/1½ lb lean lamb (leg or shoulder, for example)
4 garlic cloves, crushed
1 teaspoon salt
4 tablespoons light soy sauce
4 tablespoons Chinese wine or dry sherry
1 whole star anise
25 g/1 oz gelatine
6 tablespoons water
2 spring onions, cut into short lengths
oil for greasing

Cut the lamb into 2.5 cm/1 inch cubes. Place in a saucepan with the garlic, salt, soy sauce, wine or sherry, star anise and enough cold water to just cover. Bring to the boil slowly and skim off any scum that rises to the surface. Cover and cook on a low heat for 2 hours or until the lamb is very tender. Drain, reserving the cooking liquid. Discard the garlic and star anise. Strain the liquid through a sieve lined with clean muslin.

Soak the gelatine in the cold water. Arrange the pieces of spring onion in the base of a greased 900 g/2 lb loaf tin. Reheat the reserved cooking liquid without boiling. Add the soaked gelatine and stir over a low heat until it dissolves. Cool the liquid, pour a little over the spring onions and place the tin in the refrigerator to set the liquid.

Combine the lamb with the remaining liquid and pour into the tin. Leave in a cool place to set completely. Turn out on to a flat plate to serve.

138 STIR-FRIED LAMB WITH NOODLES

Preparation time:
15 minutes

Cooking time:
8 minutes

Serves 4-6

Calories:
330-220 per portion

YOU WILL NEED:
100 g/4 oz cellophane noodles
1 tablespoon sunflower oil
3 spring onions, chopped
1 x 2.5 cm/1 inch piece fresh root ginger, peeled and chopped
2 garlic cloves, sliced
2 celery sticks, chopped
450 g/1 lb very lean lamb, thinly sliced
1 red pepper, cored, seeded and sliced
2 tablespoons light soy sauce
2 tablespoons Chinese wine or dry sherry
150 ml/¼ pint Chinese stock (see recipe 2)
2 teaspoons sesame oil

Soak the noodles in warm water for about 10 minutes; drain.

Heat the oil in a wok or frying pan over a moderate heat. Add the spring onions, ginger and garlic and stir-fry for 1 minute. Add the celery and lamb and cook for 2 minutes. Add the red pepper, soy sauce and wine or sherry and bring to the boil. Stir in the stock and noodles and simmer for 5 minutes. Sprinkle with the sesame oil and serve at once.

■ COOK'S TIP

Most of the Chinese lamb dishes come from the northern area around the city of Peking. Jellied lamb can be served with a selection of other cold meats either as the main part of the meal or as an appetizer.

■ COOK'S TIP

To slice meat thinly you will need sharp, good quality knives and a solid chopping board. If the meat is slightly frozen it will be much easier to cut.

139 STIR-FRIED GARLIC LAMB

Preparation time:
5 minutes, plus
marinating

Cooking time:
5 minutes

Serves 4

Calories:
220 per portion

YOU WILL NEED:
350 g/12 oz lamb fillet
2 tablespoons Chinese wine or
*   dry sherry*
2 tablespoons light soy sauce
1 tablespoon dark soy sauce
1 teaspoon sesame oil
2 tablespoons sunflower oil
6 garlic cloves, thinly sliced
1 x 2.5 cm/1 inch piece fresh root
*   ginger, peeled and chopped*
1 leek, thinly sliced diagonally
4 spring onions, chopped

Cut the lamb into thin slices across the grain. Mix the wine or
sherry with the soy sauces and sesame oil. Add the lamb and
toss to coat the slices thoroughly. Leave to marinate for
15 minutes. Drain, reserving the marinade.

Heat the sunflower oil in a wok or deep frying pan over a
moderate heat. Add the meat and about 2 teaspoons of the
marinade. Fry briskly for about 2 minutes until the meat is
well browned. Add the garlic, ginger, leek and spring onions
and stir-fry for a further 3 minutes. Serve at once.

140 RED-COOKED LAMB

Preparation time:
25-30 minutes

Cooking time:
1¼ hours

Serves 4-6

Calories:
477-318 per portion

YOU WILL NEED:
900 g/2 lb lean lamb fillet, cubed
4 garlic cloves, sliced
3 slices fresh root ginger, peeled and
*   finely chopped*
1 teaspoon 5-spice powder
6 tablespoons light soy sauce
3 tablespoons Chinese wine or
*   dry sherry*
6 spring onions
600 ml/1 pint beef stock
50 g/2 oz soft brown sugar
1 red pepper, cored, seeded and diced
1 green pepper, cored, seeded and diced

Place the lamb in a saucepan. Sprinkle over the garlic and
ginger and mix well. Add the 5-spice powder, soy sauce and
wine or sherry.

Cut each spring onion into 3 pieces and add to the lamb.
Pour over the stock and stir in the brown sugar. Bring to the
boil, cover and simmer for 1-1¼ hours, until the meat is
tender. Remove the lid, increase the heat and continue to cook
until the remaining liquid is reduced to a thick sauce.

Spoon the red-cooked lamb and sauce on to a warmed
serving dish. Scatter the diced red and green pepper on top
and serve immediately.

■ COOK'S TIP

*This dish is elegant in its
simplicity. Vegetable dishes
to accompany it might
include Aubergines in
fragrant sauce (recipe 166),
which is excellent with all*
*lamb dishes, or simple Fried
lettuce (recipe 182) and a
bowl of Plain boiled rice
(recipe 206).*

■ COOK'S TIP

*Red-cooking is a unique
Chinese method, used
primarily for cooking larger
cuts of meat and whole
poultry. The soy sauce gives
a rich flavour and colour.*

141 CRISPY BARBECUED PORK

Preparation time:
10 minutes, plus
standing

Cooking time:
about 1¼ hours

Oven temperature:
230 C, 450 F, gas 8
then
200 C/400 F, gas 6

Serves 6-8

Calories:
650-500 per portion

YOU WILL NEED:
1.5 kg/3 lb belly of pork, in one piece
salt
1 tablespoon light soy sauce
1 teaspoon 5-spice powder
FOR THE GARNISH
turnip flowers (see recipe 144)
radish waterlily (see recipe 98)

Pour a kettleful of boiling water over the skin of the pork, drain and dry. Rub the pork with salt and leave to dry for 45 minutes.

Score the skin of the pork in a diamond pattern. Pierce the meat with a skewer in several places. Rub the soy sauce and 5-spice powder into the pork. Cover and stand for 1 hour.

Place the pork, skin side up, in a roasting pan. Place in a preheated oven and roast at the higher temperature for 20 minutes. Reduce the heat and continue to cook for 50-55 minutes, or until the meat is tender and the skin is crisp. If necessary place the pork under a preheated grill for 1-2 minutes to crisp up the skin.

Serve hot, garnished as shown.

■ COOK'S TIP

At a Chinese meal this dish would probably be sliced before bringing it to the table, but its appearance is so mouthwatering it is worth presenting it whole.

142 PORK SLICES WITH CHINESE VEGETABLES

Preparation time:
25-30 minutes, plus
soaking

Cooking time:
10 minutes

Serves 4

Calories:
262 per portion

YOU WILL NEED:
225 g/8 oz pork fillet, thinly sliced
1 tablespoon light soy sauce
1 tablespoon Chinese wine
1 tablespoon cornflour
4-5 dried shiitake mushrooms
100 g/4 oz mangetout
100 g/4 oz water chestnuts
2 spring onions
4 tablespoons sunflower oil
100 g/4 oz bamboo shoots, thinly sliced
1 teaspoon salt
1 teaspoon sugar
2 teaspoons water

Mix the pork with the soy sauce, wine and ½ tablespoon of the cornflour. Soak the mushrooms in boiling water for 15 minutes. Drain, discard the hard stems and slice the caps. Halve the mangetout if large. Cut each water chestnut into small pieces and the spring onions into short lengths.

Heat the oil in a wok and stir-fry the pork for 1 minute or until the meat changes colour. Remove with a perforated spoon.

In the remaining oil, stir-fry the spring onions briefly. Add the mangetout, bamboo shoots, mushrooms and water chestnuts and stir-fry for 1 minute. Add the salt and sugar, then the pork. Stir-fry for 1 minute. Add the remaining cornflour with the water, to thicken the sauce.

■ COOK'S TIP

If mangetout are unavailable, substitute fresh broccoli, broken into small florets. Broccoli takes slightly longer to cook, so allow an extra minute or two before adding the bamboo shoots and other ingredients to the wok.

143 CHILLI PORK SPARERIBS

Preparation time:	YOU WILL NEED:
15 minutes	1 kg/2 lb lean pork spareribs, cut into
	5 cm/2 inch pieces
Cooking time:	salt
45 minutes	2 tablespoons sunflower oil
	2 dried red chillies
Serves 4-6	1 × 2.5 cm/1 inch piece fresh root
	ginger, peeled and finely chopped
Calories:	1 garlic clove, thinly sliced
350-240 per portion	FOR THE SAUCE
	4 tablespoons clear honey
	4 tablespoons wine vinegar
	2 tablespoons light soy sauce
	2 tablespoons dry sherry
	1 × 142 g/5 oz can tomato purée
	1 teaspoon chilli powder
	2 garlic cloves, crushed

Mix all the sauce ingredients together and set aside. Sprinkle the spareribs with salt.

Heat the oil in a wok and quickly fry the red chillies to flavour it. Remove the chillies with a slotted spoon and discard. Add the ginger and garlic to the wok and stir-fry over moderate heat for 30 seconds. Add the spareribs and stir-fry for 5 minutes, until golden brown. Reduce the heat and cook gently for 10 minutes.

Add the sauce to the wok, cover and simmer gently for 25-30 minutes. Serve hot.

144 BRAISED LEG OF PORK

Preparation time:	YOU WILL NEED:
10-15 minutes	1 × 1.5-1.76 kg/3-4 lb leg of pork
	salt
Cooking time:	6 spring onions
3 hours	2 slices fresh root ginger, peeled
	and chopped
Serves 6-8	150 ml/ ¼ pint light soy sauce
	6 tablespoons Chinese wine or
Calories:	dry sherry
464-348 per portion	50 g/2 oz soft brown sugar
	FOR THE GARNISH
	radish waterlilies (see recipe 98)
	turnip flowers (see Cook's Tip)
	spring onions

Rub the pork with salt; do not score the skin. Cut the spring onions into 3 pieces and place them in a large saucepan with the ginger, soy sauce and wine or sherry. Stir in the sugar and add the pork, turning to coat it with the mixture. Bring to the boil over moderate heat, cover and simmer for 2-2½ hours, until very tender, turning occasionally.

Remove the pork from the pan and keep it hot. Boil the sauce until it is well reduced and thickened. Pour into a sauce bowl. Carve the meat into thick slices and arrange on a serving dish. Garnish with the radish waterlilies, turnip flowers and spring onions and serve hot or cold, with the sauce.

▨ COOK'S TIP

Spareribs make a delicious starter. Provide small bowls of warm water and plenty of paper napkins whenever serving food that is eaten with the fingers.

▨ COOK'S TIP

To make turnip flowers, thinly pare a strip from a whole peeled turnip, taking care to keep it in one piece. Tightly curl into a circle to make a flower.

145 TWICE-COOKED PORK WITH CHILLI BEAN SAUCE

Preparation time:	YOU WILL NEED:
15 minutes	350 g/12 oz belly pork in one piece
	100 g/4 oz bamboo shoots
Cooking time:	100 g/4 oz celery sticks
35-40 minutes	3 tablespoons sunflower oil
	2 spring onions, chopped
Serves 3-4	1 garlic clove, chopped
	2 tablespoons sake or dry sherry
Calories:	1 tablespoon light soy sauce
550-400 per portion	1 tablespoon chilli bean paste

Place the whole piece of pork in a pan of boiling water and cook for 25-30 minutes. Remove and leave to cool.

Cutting across the grain, slice the meat thinly into pieces not much larger than a postage stamp. Cut the bamboo shoots and celery into 5 cm/2 inch chunks.

Heat the oil in a wok or deep frying pan until smoking. Add the spring onions and garlic to flavour the oil, then add the vegetables and stir-fry briefly. Add the pork, then the sake or sherry, soy sauce and chilli bean sauce. Stir-fry for 2 minutes. Transfer to a warmed dish and serve immediately with an accompaniment of noodles.

146 FRIED PORK LIVER

Preparation time:	YOU WILL NEED:
5 minutes, plus	225 g/8 oz pig's liver
soaking	1 tablespoon light soy sauce
	1 tablespoon cornflour
Cooking time:	2-3 dried shiitake mushrooms
4 minutes	4 tablespoons sunflower oil
	100 g/4 oz onions, thinly sliced
Serves 4	1 teaspoon salt
	1 tablespoon Chinese wine or
Calories:	dry sherry
256 per portion	1 teaspoon sugar
	3 tablespoons Chinese stock (see
	recipe 2) or water
	1 teaspoon sesame oil

Cut the liver into 5 cm/2 inch squares about 1 cm/½ inch thick. Place in a bowl and sprinkle over the soy sauce and the cornflour. Turn to coat the pieces evenly.

Soak the mushrooms in boiling water for 15 minutes. Drain, discard the hard stems and quarter the caps.

Heat 2 tablespoons of the oil in a wok or frying pan over high heat. Stir-fry the liver very briefly, just until the pieces have separated. Remove from the wok with a slotted spoon.

Heat the remaining oil in the wok and when it is hot stir in the sliced onions and mushrooms. Return the liver to the wok, add the salt, wine or sherry and sugar and stir to blend. Add a little stock or water and stir for 30 seconds to thicken the sauce. Sprinkle over the sesame oil, transfer to a warmed dish and serve immediately.

COOK'S TIP

Belly of pork is ideal for this recipe which uses two cooking methods — 'cross-cooking' — first boiling and then frying to ensure full flavour and a crisp texture.

COOK'S TIP

Quick cooking is the best way to ensure that liver has a tender texture when cooked. As with all stir-fried dishes, it is important to cut the ingredients to small, even slices or pieces before you begin.

147 STIR-FRIED PORK AND MANGETOUT

Preparation time:
15 minutes, plus
marinating and
soaking

Cooking time:
6 minutes

Serves 4-6

Calories:
188-125 per portion

YOU WILL NEED:
350 g/12 oz lean pork, thinly sliced
2 tablespoons light soy sauce
2 tablespoons Chinese wine or
    dry sherry
4 dried shiitake mushrooms
1 tablespoon sunflower oil
225 g/8 oz mangetout

Place the sliced pork in a bowl with the soy sauce and wine or sherry. Turn the slices to coat them thoroughly, then leave to marinate for 15 minutes.

Soak the dried mushrooms in boiling water for 15 minutes. Drain, discard the hard stalks and slice the caps.

Heat the oil in a wok or frying pan over a moderate heat. Add the pork and marinade and stir-fry for 2 minutes. Add the mushrooms and stir-fry for 1 minute. Finally add the mangetout and stir-fry for a further 2 minutes.

Transfer to a warmed serving dish and serve immediately.

148 GRILLED GINGER PORK

Preparation time:
10 minutes, plus
marinating

Cooking time:
about 35 minutes

Serves 4

Calories:
150 per portion

YOU WILL NEED:
2 pork fillets, each weighing
    175-225 g/6-8 oz
1 x 5 cm/2 inch piece fresh root ginger,
    peeled and grated
4 tablespoons soy sauce
grated mooli, to garnish (see
    Cook's Tip)

Place the pork fillets in a shallow dish, add the ginger and soy sauce and leave to marinate for at least 30 minutes.

Wrap each fillet in foil, reserving the marinade. Place the wrapped pork under a preheated hot grill for 5 minutes, then turn the grill down to low and cook for a further 20-25 minutes or until thoroughly cooked.

Unwrap the pork and cut each fillet into 1 cm/½ inch slices. Place on warmed individual plates. Pour the meat juices from the foil into a pan and add the reserved marinade. If there is not enough sauce add a few spoonfuls of water and light soy sauce to taste. Bring to the boil and simmer for 5 minutes. Divide the sauce between 4 small bowls, one for each guest. Garnish the pork with grated mooli and serve with steamed green beans.

▨ COOK'S TIP

The appearance of this dish is enhanced if the slices of meat and mushrooms are the same size and shape as the mangetout; try to obtain large mushrooms if you can.

If Chinese mushrooms are not available, fresh large-cap mushrooms can be substituted.

▨ COOK'S TIP

The mooli is a long white radish with a crisp texture, widely used in Oriental cookery as a garnish.

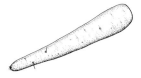

149 PORK MEATBALLS WITH VEGETABLES

Preparation time:
20 minutes

Cooking time:
about 35 minutes

Serves 4

Calories:
350 per portion

YOU WILL NEED:
450 g/1 lb minced pork
2 tablespoons light soy sauce
1 tablespoon Chinese wine or
   dry sherry
1¼ teaspoons sugar
1 egg, beaten
1 tablespoon cornflour
3-4 dried shiitake mushrooms
3 tablespoons sunflower oil
2 slices fresh root ginger, peeled
   and shredded
2 spring onions, chopped
225 g/8 oz Chinese cabbage or greens,
   cut into small pieces
1 teaspoon salt
100 g/4 oz cellophane noodles
3 tablespoons Chinese stock (see
   recipe 2) or water

Mix the pork with the soy sauce, wine or sherry, sugar, egg and cornflour. Divide and shape into 12 meatballs.

Prepare the mushrooms (see recipe 6).

Heat the oil in a frying pan and fry the meatballs until golden. Remove and set aside. Add the ginger and spring onion to the pan, then the cabbage and mushrooms. Fry 1-2 minutes. Stir in the salt, and add the meatballs and noodles. Moisten with the stock or water and bring to the boil. Reduce the heat, cover and simmer 20-25 minutes.

▓ COOK'S TIP

Ready-minced pork is sometimes available in supermarkets. If not, buy meat from the neck end and ask the butcher to mince it for you.

150 AUBERGINE AND PORK IN HOT SAUCE

Preparation time:
10 minutes, plus
standing

Cooking time:
about 10 minutes

Serves 4

Calories:
230 per portion

YOU WILL NEED:
175 g/6 oz boned lean pork, shredded
2 spring onions, chopped
1 slice fresh root ginger, peeled and
chopped
1 garlic clove, chopped
1 tablespoon light soy sauce
2 teaspoons sake or dry sherry
1 ½ teaspoons cornflour
oil for deep-frying
225 g/8 oz aubergine, cut into
diamond-shaped chunks
1 tablespoon chilli sauce
3-4 tablespoons chicken stock or water
chopped spring onions, to garnish

Place the pork in a bowl with the spring onions, ginger, garlic, soy sauce, sake or sherry and cornflour. Mix well to coat the pieces and leave to stand for 20 minutes.

Heat the oil to 180 C/350 F or until a cube of day-old bread browns in 30 seconds. Deep-fry the aubergine for 1½ minutes. Remove with a slotted spoon and drain on absorbent kitchen paper.

Pour off all but 1 tablespoon of oil from the pan. Add the pork mixture and stir-fry for 2 minutes. Add the aubergine and chilli sauce and cook for 1½ minutes, then moisten with stock or water. Simmer until the liquid has almost completely evaporated. Serve hot, garnished with chopped spring onions.

▓ COOK'S TIP

Aubergines can be bitter unless salted before cooking. Cut or slice as directed and dust all over with salt. Let stand for 30 minutes, rinse in cold water and pat dry.

151 MU-SHU PORK SHANDONG STYLE

Preparation time:	YOU WILL NEED:
20-25 minutes, plus soaking	175-225 g/6-8 oz pork fillet
	3 dried shiitake mushrooms
	2 spring onions
Cooking time:	3 eggs
8 minutes	1 teaspoon salt
	4 tablespoons sunflower oil
Serves 4	225 g/8 oz hard white cabbage, finely shredded
Calories:	1 tablespoon light soy sauce
213 per portion	1 tablespoon Chinese wine or dry sherry

Slice the pork into matchstick-sized segments. Soak the mushrooms in boiling water for 15 minutes. Drain, discard the hard stalks and shred the caps thinly. Cut the spring onions into short lengths.

Lightly beat the eggs with a pinch of the salt. Heat 1 tablespoon of the oil in a wok or frying pan and scramble the eggs until lightly set. Remove the scrambled eggs from the wok.

Wipe the wok with absorbent kitchen paper, heat the remaining oil over a high heat and stir-fry the shredded pork for 30 seconds. Add the cabbage, mushrooms and spring onions, stir-fry briefly and add the remaining salt, the soy sauce and wine or sherry. Stir-fry for 1-1½ minutes more, then return the eggs to the wok, stirring to break them into shreds. Serve the dish as soon as the ingredients are nicely blended.

152 STEAMED STUFFED AUBERGINES

Preparation time:	YOU WILL NEED:
15 minutes	1 tablespoon sunflower oil
	2 garlic cloves, crushed
Cooking time:	1 x 2.5 cm/1 inch piece fresh root ginger, peeled and chopped
about 1 hour	4 spring onions, chopped
Serves 4-6	2 red or green fresh chillies, seeded and chopped
Calories:	225 g/8 oz minced pork
190-130 per portion	2 tablespoons light soy sauce
	2 tablespoons Chinese wine or dry sherry
	4 medium aubergines
	50 g/2 oz peeled prawns

Heat the oil in a wok or deep frying pan over moderate heat. Add the garlic, ginger and spring onions and stir-fry for 1 minute. Increase the heat, add the chillies and pork and cook for 10 minutes.

Meanwhile, halve the aubergines lengthways, carefully scoop out the flesh and chop finely. Add the flesh to the pan and cook for 10 minutes. Stir in the prawns and cook for 1 minute.

Blanch the aubergine shells in boiling water for 1 minute. Drain and stuff with the meat mixture. Place in a dish in a steamer and steam vigorously for 25-30 minutes. Serve immediately.

▓ COOK'S TIP

Mu-shu is the Chinese name for cassia, a fragrant yellow flower that blooms in the autumn. Egg dishes in China are often given the name Mu-shu because of the bright yellow colour. Traditionally this dish is eaten as a filling wrapped in thin pancakes (see recipe 217) for a main course, but it can also be served as a hot starter.

▓ COOK'S TIP

To scoop out the flesh of aubergines, first cut them in half and then criss-cross through with a sharp knife without penetrating the skin. Carefully cut out the flesh.

153 BRAISED PORK WITH BAMBOO SHOOTS AND MUSHROOMS

Preparation time:
10 minutes, plus
soaking

Cooking time:
about 25 minutes

Serves 4

Calories:
500 per portion

YOU WILL NEED:
4 medium dried shiitake mushrooms
2 tablespoons sunflower oil
3 slices fresh root ginger, peeled
and chopped
1 spring onion, chopped
675 g/1 ½ lb pork shoulder, cubed
2 tablespoons Chinese wine or
dry sherry
2 tablespoons light soy sauce
1 × 227 g/8 oz can bamboo shoots,
drained and chopped
2 teaspoons garlic salt
1 teaspoon sugar
300 ml/ ½ pint water

Soak the mushrooms in boiling water for 20 minutes. Drain, discard the hard stems and quarter the caps.

Heat the oil in a wok or frying pan over moderate heat and stir-fry the ginger and spring onion for 30 seconds. Add the pork and stir-fry for 2 minutes or until lightly browned. Add the wine or sherry and soy sauce and stir for 1 minute. Add the bamboo shoots and mushrooms and stir-fry for 30 seconds. Add the garlic salt, sugar and water, bring to the boil, cover and simmer for 20 minutes. Transfer to a warmed serving dish and serve hot.

154 KIDNEY SALAD

Preparation time:
15-20 minutes, plus
marinating

Cooking time:
5 minutes

Serves 4

Calories:
86 per portion

YOU WILL NEED:
2 pig's kidneys (approx 225 g/8 oz
total weight)
600 ml/1 pint boiling water
2 slices fresh root ginger, peeled
and thinly shredded
1 spring onion, chopped, to garnish
FOR THE SAUCE
½ teaspoon salt
2 tablespoons Chinese wine or
dry sherry
1 tablespoon sesame oil

Peel off the thin white skin covering the kidneys. Split them in half lengthways and discard the fat and tough central part. Score the surface of the kidneys diagonally in a criss-cross pattern, then cut them into thin slices.

Place the kidney slices in a pan with the boiling water over a moderate heat to blanch them. As soon as the water comes back to the boil, remove the kidneys with a slotted spoon and place under cold running water for a few seconds. Place on a serving dish and toss with the shredded ginger.

Mix together the ingredients for the sauce and pour it evenly over the kidneys. Leave to marinate for at least 15 minutes. Garnish with spring onion and serve cold.

COOK'S TIP

For a particularly luxurious texture, use tenderloin of pork instead of the pork shoulder, remembering that very lean cuts may need an increase in cooking liquid.

COOK'S TIP

A popular and colourful variation on this dish includes 225 g/8 oz cooked chicken breast meat, finely chopped, and 175 g/6 oz diced ham, with a scattering *of diced green pepper on top.*

155 CASSEROLE OF LION'S HEAD

Preparation time:
20 minutes

Cooking time:
25-30 minutes

Serves 4-6

Calories:
400-260 per portion

YOU WILL NEED:
675 g/1½ lb finely minced pork
1 teaspoon salt
2 garlic cloves, crushed
1 x 5 cm/2 inch piece fresh root ginger,
    peeled and chopped
4 tablespoons light soy sauce
3 tablespoons Chinese wine or
    dry sherry
4 spring onions, chopped
1 tablespoon cornflour
oil for deep frying
300 ml/ ½ pint beef stock
675 g/1½ lb fresh spinach
chopped spring onion, to garnish

Mix the pork with the salt, garlic, ginger and 1 tablespoon each of the soy sauce and wine or sherry. Add half of the chopped spring onions. Mix in the cornflour and divide the mixture into balls the size of a walnut.

Heat the oil in a wok or deep-frier to 160 C/325°F or until a cube of day-old bread browns in 45 seconds. Deep-fry the pork balls until golden. Drain well, then place in a clean pan with the remaining soy sauce, wine or sherry and spring onions. Spoon over the stock, cover and simmer for 15-20 minutes.

Wash the spinach leaves and cook in just the water clinging to the leaves. When tender, drain well and transfer to a warmed serving dish. Arrange the meatballs on top and garnish with chopped spring onion. Serve at once.

COOK'S TIP

Lion's Head meatballs are an Eastern Chinese dish. They are usually served with noodles arranged on top like a lion's mane.

156 PORK CHOP SUEY

Preparation time:
20-25 minutes

Cooking time:
6 minutes

Serves 4

Calories:
284 per portion

YOU WILL NEED:
225 g/8 oz pork fillet
2 tablespoons light soy sauce
1 tablespoon Chinese wine or
    dry sherry
2 teaspoons cornflour
2 spring onions
100 g/4 oz fresh beansprouts
5 tablespoons sunflower oil
1 slice fresh root ginger, peeled
    and finely chopped
fresh vegetables (see Cook's Tip)
2 teaspoons salt
1 tablespoon sugar
2 tablespoons Chinese stock (see
    recipe 2) or water

Cut the pork into small, postage stamp slices. Place in a bowl and sprinkle over the soy sauce, wine or sherry and cornflour. Mix together so that the meat is evenly coated.

Cut the spring onions into 2.5 cm/1 inch lengths. Wash the beansprouts in cold water, discarding any particles that rise tothe surface of the water. Drain.

Heat 3 tablespoons of the oil in a wok over high heat. Stir-fry the pork for 1 minute or until the pieces separate. Remove and set aside. Add the remaining oil to the wok and stir-fry the spring onions and ginger for 30 seconds. Add the vegetables one by one, stir-frying briefly after each addition. Stir in salt and sugar and return the pork to the wok. Moisten with stock or water. Transfer to a warmed dish to serve.

COOK'S TIP

This is a basic recipe for cooking pork, chicken, beef or prawns with vegetables (usually several different kinds, which can be varied according to seasonal availability). Suggested vegetables: green pepper, cauliflower, tomatoes, carrots and green beans, all cut in similarly sized pieces.

157 STIR-FRIED PORK WITH BAMBOO SHOOTS

Preparation time:
25-30 minutes

Cooking time:
about 5 minutes

Serves 4

Calories:
220 per portion

YOU WILL NEED:
4 dried shiitake mushrooms
225 g/8 oz pork fillet
2 tablespoons soy sauce
1 tablespoon cornflour
225 g/8 oz bamboo shoots
4 tablespoons sunflower oil
1½ teaspoons salt
2 tablespoons Chinese wine or
* dry sherry*
spring onion tassels, to garnish (see
* recipe 33)*

Soak the mushrooms in boiling water for 20 minutes. Drain, discard the hard stalks and halve or quarter the caps, depending on size. Retain the soaking liquid.

Cut the pork into thin slices about the size of a postage stamp. Mix together the soy sauce and cornflour, then add the pork and toss to coat the pieces. Cut the bamboo shoots into thin slices the same size as the pork.

Heat 2 tablespoons of the oil in a wok over moderate heat and stir-fry the pork slices for about 1 minute, or until lightly coloured. Remove with a slotted spoon and set aside.

Add the remaining oil and increase the heat. Add the mushrooms and bamboo shoots, then the salt, pork and wine. Cook a further 1-2 minutes, stirring. If necessary, add a little mushroom liquid. Transfer to a serving dish and serve hot, garnished with spring onion tassels.

158 CRYSTAL-BOILED PORK WITH DIP SAUCE

Preparation time:
15-20 minutes

Cooking time:
1¼ hours

Serves 4

Calories:
259 per portion

YOU WILL NEED:
750g/1½-1¼ lb leg of pork, boned but
* not skinned*
spring onion tassels, to garnish (see
* recipe 33)*
FOR THE SAUCE
4 tablespoons light soy sauce
1 tablespoon sesame oil
1 teaspoon finely chopped spring onion
1 teaspoon finely chopped fresh
* root ginger*
½ teaspoon finely chopped garlic
1 teaspoon chilli sauce (optional)

Place the pork in one piece (tied together with string if necessary) in a saucepan of boiling water. Skim off the scum, cover and simmer gently for 1 hour. Remove the pork and soak it in cold water for 1 minute.

To serve, remove the string and cut off the skin, leaving a thin layer of fat covering the meat. Cut the meat across the grain into small thin slices. Put any uneven pieces in the centre of a serving dish. Arrange some of the slices in two neat rows on either side and arrange the remainder neatly in a third row on top. Garnish with spring onion tassels.

Mix together all the ingredients for the sauce, which can be poured over the meat, or served separately as a dip.

COOK'S TIP

All cooking traditions recognize the affinity between pork and cabbage. This dish goes well with Chinese cabbage casserole (recipe 175) – but omit the ham – since it does not require any last minute attention.

COOK'S TIP

This is a beautiful dish for a buffet supper party. Serve with Prawn cutlets (recipe 74), Crispy pancake rolls (recipe 218) and a selection of pickled vegetables.

159 FRIED PORK WITH BABY CORN

Preparation time:
5 minutes

Cooking time:
about 5 minutes

Serves 4

Calories:
260 per portion

YOU WILL NEED:
1 tablespoon Chinese wine or
   dry sherry
1 tablespoon light soy sauce
1½ teaspoons cornflour
450 g/1 lb pork fillet, sliced as thinly
   as possible
1 tablespoon sunflower oil
450 g/1 lb baby corn
1 teaspoon salt
50 g/2 oz mangetout
1 x 425 g/15 oz can straw mushrooms,
   drained
2 teaspoons sugar
2 teaspoons water

Mix the wine or sherry and soy sauce with 1 teaspoon of the cornflour. Add the pork and toss to coat well.

Heat the oil in a wok or frying pan and stir-fry the pork until it is lightly browned. Add the baby corn and salt and stir-fry for 30 seconds. Add the mangetout and mushrooms and stir-fry for 1 minute. Sprinkle in the sugar.

Mix the remaining cornflour with the water to make a thin paste and add this to the wok, stirring until the sauce is thickened. Transfer to a warmed serving dish and serve at once, while hot.

160 THAI-FRIED PORK BALLS

Preparation time:
20 minutes

Cooking time:
about 12 minutes

Serves 4

Calories:
320 per portion

YOU WILL NEED:
2 coriander roots, finely chopped
2 teaspoons black pepper
4 garlic cloves
pinch of sugar
450 g/1 lb minced pork
2 tablespoons nam pla (fish sauce)
flour for dredging
4-5 tablespoons sunflower oil
fresh coriander leaves, to garnish

Put the coriander roots, pepper, garlic and sugar in a blender or food processor and work to a paste. Add the pork and mix well. Add the fish sauce, blending well, then divide the mixture into 20 balls the size of a walnut. Dust with the flour.

Heat the oil in a wok or frying pan over a moderate heat. Fry the meatballs in batches of 5 for 2-3 minutes, or until no liquid is released from the balls when pierced with a skewer. Pile into a warmed serving dish and garnish with fresh coriander leaves. Serve hot.

▓ COOK'S TIP

Baby corn cobs are available in cans and need half the cooking time of fresh corn. Look out for other fresh baby vegetables such as carrots and cauliflower.

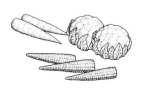

▓ COOK'S TIP

The cooking of Thailand and south China has much in common. Because food is often highly seasoned and spicy, rice is usually cooked without salt, to act as a foil for the flavourful dishes.

161 SZECHUAN DRY-FRIED SHREDDED BEEF

Preparation time:
20-25 minutes

Cooking time:
15 minutes

Serves 4

Calories:
194 per portion

YOU WILL NEED:
275 g/10 oz frying steak (rump or fillet)
100 g/4 oz carrots
2 tablespoons sesame oil
2 tablespoons Chinese wine
1 tablespoon chilli bean paste
1 tablespoon hoisin sauce
1 garlic clove, finely chopped
½ teaspoon salt
1 tablespoon sugar
2 spring onions, finely chopped
2 slices fresh root ginger, peeled
    and finely chopped
½ teaspoon freshly ground Szechuan
    or black pepper
1 teaspoon chilli oil

Cut the steak into thin shreds the size of matchsticks, then cut the carrots to the same size.

Heat a wok or frying pan over a high heat for 1 minute. Add the sesame oil and reduce the heat to moderate. Add the steak with 1 tablespoon of the wine. Stir to separate the shreds then reduce the heat. Pour off any excess liquid and continue to cook, stirring gently until the meat is dry. Add the chilli bean paste, hoisin sauce, garlic, salt, sugar and remaining wine. Stir-fry for 1 minute.

Increase the heat to high, add the shredded carrots and stir-fry for 2 minutes. Add the spring onions, ginger, pepper and chilli oil and stir once or twice to blend.

▓ COOK'S TIP

Dry-frying is a cooking method unique to Szechuan cuisine. Its principle distinctive feature is that the main ingredients are first slowly stir-fried over a low heat with seasonings, then finished off with supplementary ingredients quickly over a high heat.

162 FRIED BEEF WITH BEANS

Preparation time:
15 minutes, plus marinating

Cooking time:
5 minutes

Serves 4

Calories:
239 per portion

YOU WILL NEED:
225 g/8 oz lean steak
2 tablespoons light soy sauce
1 tablespoon cornflour
225 g/8 oz French beans
4 tablespoons sunflower oil
1 teaspoon salt
1 tablespoon Chinese wine or
    dry sherry
1-2 tablespoons Chinese stock (see
    recipe 2) or water
shredded spring onion, to garnish

Cut the meat into matchstick-sized shreds. Mix together the soy sauce and cornflour and combine with the shredded meat. Leave to marinate for 10 minutes.

Cut the beans into 5 cm/2 inch lengths.

Heat 2 tablespoons of the oil in a wok or frying pan over a high heat. Stir-fry the meat for about 1 minute or until lightly coloured. Remove with a slotted spoon and set aside.

Heat the remaining oil in the wok and stir-fry the beans with the salt for 1-1½ minutes. Add the meat and the wine or sherry. Blend well together and add a little stock or water. Do not overcook – the beans should be crisp and the meat tender. Serve hot, garnished with strips of spring onion.

▓ COOK'S TIP

A wok is the perfect utensil for stir-frying as the heat is evenly distributed and the ingredients constantly return to the centre, however vigorously you stir them.

163 STUFFED PEPPERS

Preparation time:
20 minutes

Cooking time:
about 40 minutes

Serves 4

Calories:
470 per portion

YOU WILL NEED:
5 tablespoons sunflower oil
1 spring onion, finely chopped
1 teaspoon 5-spice powder
2 teaspoons chilli paste
350 g/12 oz lean minced beef
3 tablespoons long-grain rice
salt
4 large green or red peppers, sliced
    lengthways, cored and seeded
1 x 400 g/14 oz can tomatoes

Heat 3 tablespoons of the oil in a wok. Add the onion and stir-fry until golden. Add the 5-spice powder and chilli paste and cook for 1 minute. Add the minced beef and stir-fry until evenly browned. Add the rice and salt to taste and stir-fry for a further 2 minutes. Leave to cool, then fill the pepper shells with this mixture.

Heat the remaining oil in a pan just large enough to hold the peppers. Pour a little of the tomato juice into each pepper. Place the remaining juice in the pan with the tomatoes, seasoning with salt to taste. Bring to simmering point, cover and cook for about 25 minutes, until the rice is tender. Serve the stuffed peppers hot.

164 STIR-FRIED SESAME BEEF

Preparation time:
5 minutes, plus
marinating

Cooking time:
6 minutes

Serves 4

Calories:
350 per portion

YOU WILL NEED:
350 g/12 oz rump steak
1 tablespoon light soy sauce
1 tablespoon dark soy sauce
1 tablespoon soft brown sugar
1 teaspoon sesame oil
1 tablespoon Chinese wine or
    dry sherry
2 tablespoons white sesame seeds
2 tablespoons sunflower oil
1 garlic clove, thinly sliced
2 celery sticks, sliced diagonally
50 g/2 oz button mushrooms, sliced

Cut the steak into thin slices, across the grain. Combine the soy sauces, sugar, sesame oil and wine or sherry. Toss the meat in this mixture and leave to marinate for 15 minutes.

Fry the sesame seeds in a dry pan until they are golden. Heat the oil in a wok or frying pan, add the garlic, celery and carrots and stir-fry briskly for 1 minute. Remove from the wok. Increase the heat, add the beef and stir-fry for about 3 minutes until well-browned. Return the vegetables to the wok, add the mushrooms and cook for a further 30 seconds. Sprinkle with the toasted sesame seeds and serve at once.

▨ COOK'S TIP

If you prefer, substitute minced pork, chicken or lamb or diced ham for the beef in this recipe. If using pork, include a few shelled shrimps as well.

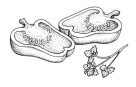

▨ COOK'S TIP

To prepare a new wok for use the protective film of oil must be removed. Heat the wok over high heat until very hot indeed, then scrub it with warm soapy water. Rinse and dry over moderate heat. Season the wok by wiping it with a pad of absorbent paper soaked in cooking oil. After each use, wash the wok without detergent.

VEGETABLE DISHES

China produces an extraordinary range of vegetables, inspiring an unrivalled variety of dishes and many cooking techniques are used. Add to this the Chinese cook's enviable choice of flavouring agents and you have delicious vegetable dishes to choose from.

165 STIR-FRIED MIXED VEGETABLES

Preparation time:
15-20 minutes

Cooking time:
3-4 minutes

Serves 4

Calories:
138 per portion

YOU WILL NEED:
100 g/4 oz fresh beansprouts
3 tablespoons sunflower oil
100 g/4 oz bamboo shoots, thinly sliced
100 g/4 oz mangetout
100 g/4 oz carrots, thinly sliced
1 teaspoon salt
1 teaspoon sugar
1 tablespoon Chinese stock (see recipe 2) or water

Wash the beansprouts in cold water, discarding the husks and small particles that rise to the surface.

Heat the oil in a wok or frying pan over moderate heat. Add the bamboo shoots, mangetout and carrots and stir-fry for 1 minute. Add the beansprouts with the salt and sugar. Stir for 1-2 minutes, and add a little stock or water if necessary. Do not overcook, as the vegetables should retain their crunchy texture. Serve hot.

166 AUBERGINES IN FRAGRANT SAUCE

Preparation time:
20 minutes

Cooking time:
5-10 minutes

Serves 4

Calories:
220 per portion

YOU WILL NEED:
225 g/8 oz aubergines
100 g/4 oz pork fillet
600 ml/1 pint sunflower oil for deep-frying
2 spring onions, finely chopped
1 slice fresh root ginger, peeled and finely chopped
1 garlic clove, finely chopped
1 tablespoon light soy sauce
1 tablespoon Chinese wine or dry sherry
2 teaspoons chilli purée
2 tablespoons cornflour
3 tablespoons water

Peel the aubergines and cut them into strips about the size of potato chips. Cut the pork into thin shreds.

Heat the oil in a wok or deep frying pan over moderate heat and deep-fry the aubergines for 1-2 minutes. Remove from the oil with a slotted spoon and drain.

Pour off all but 1 tablespoon of oil from the wok. Over a high heat, quickly stir-fry the spring onions, ginger and garlic. Add the pork and stir-fry for 1 minute. Add the soy sauce, wine or sherry and chilli purée, blending well. Add the aubergines and cook for 1-2 minutes.

Mix the cornflour with the water to make a thin paste. Add this to the wok, stirring until the sauce is thickened.

▓COOK'S TIP

When stir-frying, choose the freshest vegetables available. Do not prepare them hours before use, and wash them before cutting them up in order to avoid losing vitamins in water. Do not overcook, and avoid using a lid over the wok or pan unless specified, as it will spoil the brightness of the colour.

▓COOK'S TIP

This dish makes a meal on its own with a bowl of rice and a serving of Sweet and sour cucumber (recipe 224). Substitute lamb fillet for the pork as a variation.

167 STEAMED CHINESE CABBAGE

Preparation time:
10 minutes

Cooking time:
35-40 minutes

Serves 4-6

Calories:
180-120 per portion

YOU WILL NEED:
675 g/1½ lb Chinese cabbage
225 g/8 oz cooked ham
2 tablespoons sunflower oil
4 tablespoons chopped spring onions
1 teaspoon salt
2 teaspoons cornflour
2 teaspoons water

Discard the tough outer leaves of the cabbage, separate the stalks, wash and cut into 10 x 15 cm/4 x 6 inch pieces. Cut the ham into pieces the same size as the cabbage.

Heat the oil in a wok, add the cabbage and stir-fry lightly. Remove from the heat. Lightly oil a heatproof bowl, then sprinkle in the spring onions. Arrange the cabbage and ham in alternate layers in the bowl. Add the salt, cover and steam over a high heat for 30 minutes.

Drain the juice from the bowl into a pan. Mix the cornflour with the water to make a thin paste and add this to the juice. Simmer, stirring, until the sauce has thickened. Arrange the ham, cabbage and spring onions on a serving plate. Pour the sauce over and serve hot.

168 CRISPY VEGETABLES

Preparation time:
15 minutes

Cooking time:
20 minutes

Serves 6

Calories:
230 per portion

YOU WILL NEED:
100 g/4 oz plain flour
pinch of salt
1 tablespoon sunflower oil
150 ml/ ¼ pint water
2 egg whites, stiffly whisked
450 g/1 lb mixed vegetables (see Cook's Tip)
oil for deep-frying
FOR THE DIP
1-2 garlic cloves, chopped
4 tomatoes, peeled, seeded and chopped
1 teaspoon chilli powder
2 avocado pears, peeled and stoned
1 tablespoon freshly chopped coriander
pinch of ground coriander (optional)

To make the dip, place all the ingredients in a blender and work to a smooth purée. Spoon into a serving dish and chill.

To make the batter, sift the flour and salt into a bowl. Gradually beat in the oil and water, then fold in the egg white.

Heat the oil in a wok or frying pan to 180 C/350 F or until a cube of day-old bread browns in 30 seconds. Dip the vegetables in the batter, then deep-fry in batches for 2-3 minutes, until golden. Make sure the oil comes back to full heat after each batch.

Drain the vegetables on absorbent kitchen paper and serve with the dip.

■ COOK'S TIP

Presentation is important in this delicate dish with its simple sauce, to emphasize the contrast in colours as well as flavours and textures.

■ COOK'S TIP

You can use many vegetables for this dish. Try cauliflower or broccoli florets, green beans, whole mushrooms, mangetout, or strips of courgettes.

169 DEEP-FRIED GREEN BEANS

Preparation time:
5 minutes

Cooking time:
12 minutes

Serves 4

Calories:
180 per portion

YOU WILL NEED:
600 ml/1 pint oil for deep-frying
450 g/1 lb French beans, trimmed
3 garlic cloves, crushed
*1 tablespoon freshly chopped
    root ginger*
4 spring onions, chopped
4 dried red chillies
1 tablespoon yellow bean sauce
*1 tablespoon Chinese wine or
    dry sherry*
1 tablespoon dark soy sauce
pinch of sugar
1 tablespoon stock

Heat the oil in a wok or deep-frier until it sizzles when a single bean is dropped in. Deep-fry half the beans for about 3-4 minutes, until they are slightly wrinkled. Remove from the oil and drain on absorbent kitchen paper. Repeat with the remaining beans.

Transfer about 1 tablespoon of the oil to a wok or frying pan over moderate heat. Add the garlic, ginger and spring onions and stir-fry for 15 seconds. Add the chillies and cook for 30 seconds, until they turn black. Remove and discard the chillies, then add the remaining ingredients and stir-fry very briefly. Add the drained beans and stir-fry for 2 minutes, until they are hot and coated in sauce. Transfer to a warmed serving dish and serve at once.

170 STIR-FRIED SUMMER VEGETABLES

Preparation time:
20 minutes

Cooking time:
about 5 minutes

Serves 4-6

Calories:
140-90 per portion

YOU WILL NEED:
2 tablespoons sunflower oil
2 spring onions, sliced
*1 x 2.5 cm/1 inch piece fresh root
    ginger, peeled and sliced*
2 garlic cloves, sliced
2 fresh chillies, seeded and chopped
50 g/2 oz button mushrooms
100 g/4 oz baby carrots, peeled
100 g/4 oz mangetout, trimmed
100 g/4 oz French beans, trimmed
50 g/2 oz beansprouts
1 red pepper, cored, seeded and sliced
2 celery sticks, sliced
a few cauliflower florets
4 tablespoons light soy sauce
*2 tablespoons Chinese wine or
    dry sherry*
1 teaspoon sesame oil

Heat the oil in a wok over moderate heat. Add the spring onions, ginger and garlic and stir-fry for 30 seconds. Add the chillies and all the vegetables. Toss well and cook, stirring, for 2 minutes. Stir in the soy sauce and wine or sherry and cook for 2 minutes.

Sprinkle over the sesame oil, pile into a warmed serving dish and serve at once.

▦ COOK'S TIP

This dish is from the western region of China, but in all Chinese cooking long green beans are thought to be a symbol of longevity and are correspondingly popular.

This deep-fried version is a good accompaniment to whole steamed fish or roast meats.

▦ COOK'S TIP

To keep the ingredients on the move when stir-frying the Chinese use a spatula rather like an unperforated fish slice, or special, long-handled chopsticks.

171 SPICY LONG BEANS WITH FISH CAKE

Preparation time:
10 minutes

Cooking time:
10 minutes

Serves 4

Calories:
120 per portion

YOU WILL NEED:
8 long French beans or runner beans
1 block fish cake
3 tablespoons sunflower oil
2 garlic cloves, crushed
1 tablespoon chilli bean paste
150 ml/ ¼ pint water
1 teaspoon salt

Cut the beans into 5 cm/2 inch lengths, wash and drain. Slice the fish cake into lengths of a similar size.

Heat the oil in a wok or frying pan and fry the garlic until light brown. Add the chilli bean paste and cook, stirring all the time, for 1 minute.

Add the long beans and cook, stirring well, for 2-3 minutes. Add the fish cake and water. Increase the heat and stir-fry briskly for 1-2 minutes. Add salt to taste and serve immediately.

172 FOUR PRECIOUS VEGETABLES

Preparation time:
10 minutes

Cooking time:
3-4 minutes

Serves 4-6

Calories:
150-100 per portion

YOU WILL NEED:
4 tablespoons sunflower oil
100 g/4 oz bamboo shoots, cut into
   2.5 cm/1 inch pieces
100 g/4 oz carrots, thinly sliced
100 g/4 oz mushrooms
100 g/4 oz broccoli florets
1 teaspoon salt
1 teaspoon sugar
1 teaspoon sesame oil

Heat the sunflower oil in a wok set over a moderate heat. Add the bamboo shoots and carrots and stir-fry for 1-2 minutes.

Leave the mushrooms whole if they are small, halve them if large, and add to the wok with the broccoli florets. Sprinkle with salt and sugar and stir-fry together for 1-2 minutes.

Sprinkle with sesame oil and transfer to a serving dish. Serve hot or cold.

▨ COOK'S TIP

Fish cake is sold in blocks at Chinese supermarkets and can be cut or sliced according to the demands of an individual recipe. Even in small quantities, it is an excellent way of adding flavour and protein to stir-fried vegetable or noodle dishes.

▨ COOK'S TIP

It is important to cut the vegetables for this dish into similar sizes and shapes, so that they will be cooked at the same time, and can easily be eaten with chopsticks.

173 CELERY SALAD

Preparation time: 15-20 minutes	YOU WILL NEED: 1 celery stick, thinly sliced diagonally 1 small green pepper, cored, seeded and thinly sliced
Cooking time: 1-2 minutes	1 slice fresh root ginger, peeled and finely shredded, to garnish
Serves 4	FOR THE DRESSING 2 tablespoons light soy sauce
Calories: 24 per portion	1 tablespoon vinegar 1 tablespoon sesame seed oil

Place the sliced celery and green pepper in a large pan of boiling salted water for 1-2 minutes only. Drain, rinse in cold water until cool and drain again. Arrange on a serving plate.

Mix together the ingredients for the dressing. Pour over the celery and green pepper and toss lightly. Garnish with shredded ginger and serve.

174 HOT AND SOUR CABBAGE

Preparation time: 15-20 minutes	YOU WILL NEED: 3 tablespoons sunflower oil 4-6 dried red chillies
Cooking time: 3 minutes	12 Szechuan peppercorns 450 g/1 lb white cabbage, thinly shredded
Serves 4	1 green pepper, cored, seeded and thinly shredded
Calories: 178 per portion	1 red pepper, cored, seeded and thinly shredded 1 tablespoon sesame oil FOR THE SAUCE 2 tablespoons light soy sauce 2 tablespoons wine or cider vinegar 2 tablespoons sugar 1 teaspoon salt

To make the sauce, mix together the soy sauce, vinegar, sugar and salt.

Heat the oil in a wok or large frying pan over moderate heat and add the dried chillies and peppercorns. After 15 seconds, add the cabbage and the green and red peppers. Stir-fry for 1-1½ minutes, then pour in the sauce mixture and continue to cook, stirring, until well blended.

Serve either hot or cold, sprinkled with sesame oil.

▨ COOK'S TIP

A Chinese 'salad' is rarely based on raw vegetables. They are usually pickled or, as here, blanched, then refreshed in cold water and mixed in a dressing.

▨ COOK'S TIP

In this recipe the hot note is provided by the chillies; the sourness comes from the vinegar, slightly offset by the sweetness of the sugar.

175 CHINESE CABBAGE CASSEROLE

Preparation time:
15-20 minutes

Cooking time:
about 35 minutes

Serves 4

Calories:
127 per portion

YOU WILL NEED:
750 g/1½ - 1¾ lb Chinese cabbage
3-4 dried shiitake mushrooms
1 tablespoon dried shrimps
450 g/1 lb bamboo shoots or carrots,
  thinly sliced
50 g/2 oz cooked ham, thinly sliced
300 ml/ ½ pint Chinese stock (see
  recipe 2)
1 teaspoon salt
1 tablespoon Chinese wine or
  dry sherry

Discard the tough outer cabbage leaves, trim the base and cut the cabbage into 3-4 sections. Place in a flameproof casserole.

Soak the dried mushrooms and shrimps separately in boiling water for 10 minutes. Drain the mushrooms, reserving the liquid, discard the hard stalks and place the caps on top of the cabbage pieces with the drained shrimps. Place the bamboo shoots or carrots and ham on top. Pour in the stock and the reserved mushroom liquid. The cabbage will exude some liquid during cooking so make sure the casserole is not over-full. Add salt, cover and cook gently for 30 minutes over moderate heat.

Just before serving, add the wine or sherry, bring to the boil and serve hot.

176 BEANSPROUT SALAD

Preparation time:
8 minutes

Cooking time:
5 minutes

Serves 6

Calories:
111 per portion

YOU WILL NEED:
450 g/1 lb fresh beansprouts
salt
2 eggs
1 tablespoon sunflower oil
100 g/4 oz cooked ham, cut into
  thin strips
FOR THE DRESSING
2 tablespoons light soy sauce
2 tablespoons wine vinegar
1 tablespoon sesame oil
freshly ground black pepper

Wash the beansprouts under cold running water. Plunge into a large saucepan of boiling salted water and blanch for 1 minute. Drain, rinse under cold running water to cool, drain again and set aside.

Put the eggs in a bowl with a pinch of salt and beat lightly. Heat the oil in an omelette pan or heavy-based frying pan, add the eggs and make a thin omelette. Remove from the pan, leave to cool and cut the omelette into thin strips.

To serve, blend all the ingredients for the dressing together. Put the beansprouts in a bowl, pour over the dressing and toss gently to mix. Transfer the salad to a serving platter and arrange the ham and omelette strips on top. Serve cool.

▦ COOK'S TIP

This recipe is traditionally prepared in a sandpot, which is made of fireproof clay. A heavy-based flameproof casserole is an acceptable alternative.

▦ COOK'S TIP

Crunchy and refreshing, this salad is ideal for summer menus. For a complete, nicely balanced meal, serve with Duck on skewers (recipe 111) or Chilli pork spareribs (recipe 143) and Crispy fried noodles (recipe 210).

177 CHINESE CABBAGE WITH WHITE FU-YUNG SAUCE

Preparation time: about 10 minutes, plus soaking	YOU WILL NEED: 675 g/1½ lb Chinese cabbage 1 tablespoon dried shrimps 1 chicken stock cube
Cooking time: 15 minutes	300 ml/ ½ pint chicken stock FU-YUNG SAUCE 2 tablespoons cornflour 1 teaspoon salt 2 egg whites, lightly beaten
Serves 4-5	3-4 tablespoons milk
Calories: 108-86 per portion	1 tablespoon cream or butter 2 tablespoons minced chicken breast

Cut the cabbage into 7.5 x 5 cm/3 x 2 inch pieces. Soak the dried shrimps in boiling water for 10 minutes, then drain. Add the shrimps and crumbled stock cube to the stock in a large saucepan or deep frying pan with a lid. Bring to the boil, stir and simmer for 1 minute.

Add the cabbage to the pan. Stir and mix the shrimps gently with the cabbage. Cover the pan and simmer gently for 8 minutes, stirring once or twice. Drain, reserving the cooking liquid.

Add the cornflour and salt to the egg whites and beat for 30 seconds. Add the milk, cream or butter and minced chicken. Pour in the reserved stock. Stir well and pour into a small saucepan. Cook, stirring, over a moderate heat for 2-3 minutes, until thickened.

Arrange the cabbage in a deep serving dish and pour the sauce over. Serve hot.

▓ COOK'S TIP

The combination of the pale green of the Chinese cabbage and the whiteness of this sauce makes this dish an ideal partner for richer, dark meat dishes.

178 BEAN CURD WITH CHILLI SAUCE

Preparation time: 10 minutes	YOU WILL NEED: 2 cakes bean curd 4 tablespoons sunflower oil
Cooking time: about 8 minutes	5 tablespoons finely chopped onion ½ teaspooon crushed garlic 100 g/4 oz minced beef
Serves 2	3 fresh green chillies, seeded and chopped
Calories: 564 per portion	½ teaspoon sugar 3 tablespoons soy sauce 2 teaspoons cornflour 4 tablespoons water

Blanch the bean curd in boiling water for 1 minute. Drain and cut into 5 mm/ ¼ inch cubes.

Heat the oil in a pan and add the onion and garlic. Stir-fry for 1 minute, then add the minced beef. Stir-fry until evenly browned. Add the bean curd, chilli peppers, sugar and soy sauce. Bring to the boil.

Combine the cornflour with the water to make a thin paste and add to the pan, stirring until the sauce has thickened. Serve hot.

▓ COOK'S TIP

Fresh bean curd, also called tofu, is made from puréed yellow soy beans. It has the appearance of an opaque junket and is sold in square cakes that can be cut to any shape. It has little flavour of its own, but immediately takes on the flavour of other elements in a dish. It is highly valued in Oriental cooking for its nutritional content.

179 BRAISED CHINESE LEAVES WITH MUSHROOMS

Preparation time:	YOU WILL NEED:
20 minutes	450 g/1 lb Chinese leaves
	350 g/12 oz canned straw mushrooms,
Cooking time:	drained, or 225 g/8 oz fresh
5-10 minutes	button mushrooms
	4 tablespoons sunflower oil
Serves 4	2 teaspoons salt
	1 teaspoon sugar
Calories:	1 tablespoon cornflour
180 per portion	3 tablespoons water
	50 ml/2 fl oz milk

Separate and wash the leaves and cut each one in half lengthways. If using fresh mushrooms, wipe the caps (do not peel) and trim the stalks.

Heat 2 tablespoons of the oil in a wok over moderate heat. Add the Chinese leaves and stir-fry for 1 minute. Add 1½ teaspoons of the salt with the sugar and stir-fry for 1 minute. Remove the leaves and arrange neatly on a warmed serving dish. Keep hot.

Mix the cornflour to a smooth paste with the water. Heat the remaining oil in the wok until hot, add the mushrooms and remaining salt and stir-fry for 1 minute. Add the cornflour paste and the milk and stir constantly until the sauce is smooth, white, and thickened. Pour evenly over the Chinese leaves and serve at once.

180 STIR-FRIED LETTUCE WITH OYSTER SAUCE

Preparation time:	YOU WILL NEED:
10 minutes	2 cos lettuces
	2 tablespoons sunflower oil
Cooking time:	2 garlic cloves, crushed
1 minute	2 teaspoons Chinese wine or dry sherry
	1 teaspoon salt
Serves 4	½ teaspoon sugar
	2 tablespoons oyster sauce or light
Calories:	soy sauce
80 per portion	

Separate the lettuce into leaves and break into 5 cm/2 inch pieces.

Heat the oil in a wok or frying pan and add the garlic, sherry, salt, sugar and lettuce leaves. Cover and cook for 1 minute, or until the leaves have just wilted.

Drain the lettuce and arrange on a serving dish. Pour the oyster sauce on top and serve hot as a main dish, or allow to cool and serve as a salad.

▨ COOK'S TIP

Try this dish with different mushrooms according to availability. Small button mushrooms are an acceptable alternative to straw mushrooms, but for an interesting flavour use oyster mushrooms with their smooth texture and beautiful pale coffee colour.

▨ COOK'S TIP

If cos lettuces are not available, or as an attractive alternative, use little gem lettuces cut into quarters. The flavour is deliciously sweet.

181 CRISPY 'SEAWEED' WITH ALMONDS

Preparation time:
10 minutes, plus
drying

Cooking time:
5 minutes

Serves 4

Calories:
128 per portion

YOU WILL NEED:
750 g/1½ - 1¾ lb spring greens
oil for deep-frying
1 teaspoon salt
1½ teaspoons caster sugar
50 g/2 oz deep-fried split almonds,
  to garnish

Wash and dry the spring green leaves and shred them with a sharp knife to give the thinnest possible shavings. Spread them out on absorbent kitchen paper or put in a large colander to dry thoroughly for about 30 minutes.

Heat the oil in a wok or deep-frier, but before it gets too hot, turn off the heat for 30 seconds. Add the spring green shavings in several batches and turn the heat up to medium high. Stir with cooking chopsticks and when the shavings start to float to the surface, scoop them out gently with a slotted spoon and drain on absorbent kitchen paper, to remove as much of the oil as possible.

Sprinkle the salt and caster sugar evenly on top, then mix gently. Serve cold, garnished with split almonds.

182 FRIED LETTUCE

Preparation time:
5 minutes

Cooking time:
2 minutes

Serves 4

Calories:
100 per portion

YOU WILL NEED:
1 large cos lettuce
2-3 tablespoons sunflower oil
1 teaspoon salt
1 teaspoon sugar

Discard the tough outer leaves of the lettuce. Separate the leaves, wash them well and shake off any excess water. Tear the larger leaves into 2 or 3 pieces.

Heat the oil in a wok or large saucepan over a moderate heat. When it is hot, add the salt followed by the lettuce leaves and stir them vigorously in the oil as though tossing a salad. Add the sugar and continue stirring. As soon as the leaves become slightly limp transfer to a serving dish and serve immediately.

███ COOK'S TIP

The very popular 'seaweed' served in Chinese restaurants is, in fact, green cabbage. (Real seaweed is found in Japanese cooking.) Choose fresh young spring greens *with pointed heads which have not developed a heart. Often served as a starter, this recipe is also an ideal garnish for a number of dishes, particularly cold starters.*

███ COOK'S TIP

This recipe is the perfect way to use up surplus lettuce. Lightly cooked lettuce retains its fresh flavour and can be served as a contrasting note to many meat dishes.

183 FRIED LETTUCE AND PRAWNS

Preparation time:
5 minutes

Cooking time:
4 minutes

Serves 4

Calories:
134 per portion

YOU WILL NEED:
3 tablespoons sunflower oil
3 spring onions, cut into 2.5 cm/1 inch
   lengths
1 x 2.5 cm/1 inch piece fresh root
   ginger, peeled and shredded
100 g/4 oz frozen peeled prawns,
   thawed
1 large cos lettuce
1 tablespoon Chinese wine or
   dry sherry
salt

Heat the oil in a wok or deep frying pan over moderate heat. Add the spring onions and stir-fry for 30 seconds until lightly browned. Add the ginger and prawns and cook for 1 minute.

Separate the lettuce into leaves, discarding the tough outer leaves, and add to the wok with the wine or sherry and salt to taste. Stir quickly for 1-2 minutes until the lettuce leaves begin to wilt.

Arrange on a warmed serving dish and serve immediately.

184 BRAISED BAMBOO SHOOTS

Preparation time:
10-15 minutes

Cooking time:
3-5 minutes

Serves 4

Calories:
158 per portion

YOU WILL NEED:
4-5 dried shiitake mushrooms
275 g/10 oz bamboo shoots
3 tablespoons sunflower oil
2 spring onions, finely chopped
1 tablespoon Chinese wine or
   dry sherry
1 tablespoon light soy sauce
1-2 tablespoons Chinese stock (see
   recipe 2) or water
2 teaspoons cornflour
2 teaspoons water
50 g/2 oz ham, finely chopped,
   to garnish

Soak the mushrooms in boiling water for 15 minutes. Drain, discard the hard stalks and slice the caps. Cut the bamboo shoots into strips the size of potato chips.

Heat the oil in a wok or deep frying pan over a moderate heat and stir-fry the spring onions, mushrooms and bamboo shoots for 1 minute. Add the wine or sherry and soy sauce. Continue to cook for a further 1 minute, adding a little stock or water if necessary.

Mix the cornflour with the water to make a thin paste and add this to the wok, stirring until the sauce thickens. Serve at once, garnished with the chopped ham.

▓ COOK'S TIP

The pretty colours of this stir-fried dish make it a good candidate for a dinner party, especially where pork or duck is served as one of the main courses. Noodles make the best accompaniment for it.

▓ COOK'S TIP

Vegetarians can adapt this dish simply by omitting the diced ham and increasing the quantity of mushrooms. Finely sliced celery may be cooked with the vegetables.

185 BRAISED AUBERGINES

Preparation time:	YOU WILL NEED:
10 minutes	275 g/10 oz aubergines
	oil for deep-frying
Cooking time:	2 tablespoons light soy sauce
25 minutes	1 tablespoon sugar
	2 tablespoons Chinese stock (see
Serves 4	recipe 2) or water
	1 teaspoon sesame oil
Calories:	
78 per portion	

Cut the aubergines into diamond-shaped chunks.

Heat the oil in a wok or saucepan until hot and deep-fry the aubergine chunks in batches until golden. Remove with a slotted spoon and drain on absorbent kitchen paper. Pour off all but 1 tablespoon of oil from the wok. Increase the heat and return the aubergines to the pan. Add the soy sauce, sugar and the stock or water. Cook for 2 minutes, stirring occasionally and adding more water if necessary. When the juice is reduced to almost nothing, add the sesame oil, blend well and serve.

186 STIR-FRIED MUSHROOMS

Preparation time:	YOU WILL NEED:
20 minutes	50 g/2 oz small dried shiitake
	mushrooms
Cooking time:	1 tablespoon sunflower oil
12 minutes	1 teaspoon finely chopped fresh
	root ginger
Serves 4-6	2 spring onions, finely chopped
	1 garlic clove, crushed
Calories:	225 g/8 oz button mushrooms
75-45 per portion	1 × 227 g/8 oz can straw mushrooms,
	drained
	1 teaspoon chilli bean sauce or chilli
	powder
	2 teaspoons Chinese wine or dry sherry
	2 teaspoons dark soy sauce
	1 tablespoon chicken stock
	pinch of sugar
	pinch of salt
	1 teaspoon sesame oil
	fresh coriander leaves, to garnish

Soak the dried mushrooms in boiling water for 15 minutes. Drain and discard the hard stalks.

Heat the oil in a wok or deep frying pan over a moderate heat and stir-fry the ginger, spring onions and garlic for 5 seconds. Stir in the dried mushrooms and button mushrooms and cook, stirring, for 5 minutes.

Add the straw mushrooms and the remaining ingredients, mixing well, and stir-fry for 5 minutes more. Transfer to a warmed serving dish and garnish with coriander leaves.

▒ COOK'S TIP

Aubergines are a natural accompaniment to lamb dishes. Aubergines grown in China are quite small, and may be round, oval or elongated in shape.

▒ COOK'S TIP

There are a number of Chinese dishes which include a variety of mushrooms, and with the increasing choice now available a number of permutations are possible using species of different colour, size and texture in a savoury sauce.

187 CHINESE VEGETABLES

Preparation time:	YOU WILL NEED:
5 minutes	1 tablespoon sunflower oil
	4 spring onions, chopped
Cooking time:	225 g/8 oz mangetout
4 minutes	225 g/8 oz asparagus, cut into
	small pieces
Serves 4	100 g/4 oz canned water chestnuts,
	drained and sliced
Calories:	1 tablespoon light soy sauce
70 per portion	1-2 tablespoons Chinese wine or
	dry sherry
	pinch of salt
	½ teaspoon sugar
	1 teaspoon sesame oil

Heat the oil in a wok or deep frying pan over moderate heat and stir-fry the spring onions for 3 seconds. Add the mangetout, asparagus and water chestnuts, toss well in the oil and cook for 1 minute. Add the remaining ingredients and stir-fry for a further 3 minutes.

Transfer to a warmed serving dish and serve at once.

188 SPICY VEGETABLES

Preparation time:	YOU WILL NEED:
10 minutes, plus	1.2 litres/2 pints water
soaking	200 g/7 oz cellophane noodles
	8 medium dried shiitake mushrooms
Cooking time:	3 tablespoons sunflower oil
about 15 minutes	225 g/8 oz Chinese cabbage, shredded
	salt
Serves 4	1 large carrot, thinly sliced
	100 g/4 oz fresh spinach leaves, cooked
Calories:	and chopped
360 per portion	FOR THE SAUCE
	1 tablespoon sesame oil
	1 tablespoon soy sauce
	2 teaspoons sugar
	2 teaspoons sesame seeds
	½ teaspoon salt

Bring the water to the boil in a pan, add the noodles and boil for 3 minutes. Drain and set aside.

Soak the mushrooms in boiling water for 20 minutes. Drain, discard the hard stems and set the caps aside.

Heat 2 tablespoons of the oil in a pan, add the cabbage and salt to taste and fry for 2 minutes. Remove and set aside. Heat the remaining oil in the pan and stir-fry the carrot for 1 minute. Return the cabbage to the pan, add the spinach and mushrooms and stir-fry for 2 minutes.

To make the sauce, put all the ingredients in a pan over moderate heat and stir well. Bring to the boil and pour over the vegetables. Add the cellophane noodles and toss to combine the ingredients. Heat through and serve immediately.

▒ COOK'S TIP

Water chestnuts are not nuts, but tubers which are peeled to reveal the white crisp flesh inside. Available in cans, they will keep for 2 weeks covered in the refrigerator.

▒ COOK'S TIP

Composite vegetable dishes like this can be served almost as meal on their own for lunch or a snack, but make an ideal accompaniment for meat dishes such as Spiced *Leg of Lamb (recipe 136) or Crispy Barbecued Pork (recipe 141).*

189 STIR-FRIED VEGETABLE OMELETTE

Preparation time:
5 minutes

Cooking time:
10 minutes

Serves 4-6

Calories:
230-150 per portion

YOU WILL NEED:
1 tablespoon sunflower oil
1 onion, finely chopped
1 garlic clove, crushed
2 potatoes, peeled, quartered and
    finely sliced
½ green or red pepper, cored, seeded
    and finely chopped
4-6 broccoli florets
3 tomatoes, sliced
¼ cucumber, chopped
5-6 large eggs, beaten
1 heaped teaspoon freshly chopped
    parsley
pepper

Heat the oil in a large wok or frying pan, add the onion and fry, stirring, until softened. Stir in the garlic, potatoes, pepper and broccoli and stir-fry for about 6 minutes, until softened but still crisp – add a little water if they start to stick. Add the tomatoes and cucumber, stir well then spread the mixture out flat.

Pour the eggs over the vegetables and stir them through. Cook until the eggs begin to set, then place the pan under a preheated hot grill until the top has just set.

Cut the omelette into wedges and sprinkle with the parsley and pepper. Serve at once.

190 STIR-FRIED GARLIC SPINACH

Preparation time:
4-5 minutes

Cooking time:
5-6 minutes

Serves 4

Calories:
120 per portion

YOU WILL NEED:
1 kg/2 lb spinach
2 tablespoons sunflower oil
4 spring onions, chopped
1 teaspoon light soy sauce
pinch of sugar
pinch of salt
2 garlic cloves, crushed
1 teaspoon toasted sesame seeds

Wash the spinach thoroughly and remove all the stems. Drain thoroughly.

Heat the oil in a wok or frying pan over moderate heat and stir-fry the spring onions for 30 seconds. Add the spinach and stir-fry for about 2 minutes, until the leaves are coated in the oil and have wilted. Add the soy sauce, sugar, salt and garlic and continue frying for 3 minutes. Pour off any excess liquid.

Transfer to a warmed serving dish and sprinkle with the sesame seeds to serve.

▨ COOK'S TIP

Vary the vegetable components of this omelette according to the seasons. Mushrooms, cooked and drained spinach, beansprouts and mangetout are possible alternatives. Add a very little freshly chopped chilli if liked.

▨ COOK'S TIP

To keep the spinach liquid to a minimum in this dish, choose very young tender spinach, remove the stems, and keep the cooking time as brief as possible.

191 STIR-FRIED GINGER BROCCOLI

Preparation time:
3-4 minutes

Cooking time:
about 3 minutes

Serves 4

Calories:
90 per portion

YOU WILL NEED:
450 g/1 lb broccoli
salt
2 tablespoons sunflower oil
1 garlic clove, thinly sliced (optional)
1 x 2.5 cm/1 inch piece fresh root
    ginger, peeled and finely shredded
½ -1 teaspoon sesame oil

Separate the broccoli heads into small florets. Peel the stems and slice them diagonally. Blanch in boiling salted water for 30 seconds, drain well and cool rapidly under cold running water; drain thoroughly.

Heat the oil in a large wok or frying pan over moderate heat and stir-fry the garlic (if used) and ginger for 3 seconds. Add the broccoli and cook for 2 minutes. Sprinkle over the sesame oil and stir-fry for a further 30 seconds. Spoon into a serving dish and serve at once.

▓ COOK'S TIP

Ginger and broccoli make a wonderful partnership, which nicely offsets the oiliness of certain fish. Try it with red mullet, herring or mackerel recipes.

192 VEGETABLES IN TOFU DRESSING

Preparation time:
20-30 minutes

Cooking time:
10-15 minutes

Serves 4

Calories:
170 per portion

YOU WILL NEED:
3 dried shiitake mushrooms
½ fennel bulb
2 slices boiled ham
1 small carrot, peeled
50 g/2 oz French beans, trimmed
400 ml/14 fl oz chicken stock
1 tablespoon light soy sauce
2 teaspoons sugar
FOR THE DRESSING
100 g/4 oz silken tofu (bean curd)
2 tablespoons tahini (sesame seed
    paste)
2½ tablespoons sugar
1 teaspoon salt

Soak the mushrooms in boiling water for 20 minutes. Drain, discard the hard stalks and cut the caps into strips. Cut the fennel, ham, carrots and French beans into strips.

Bring the stock to the boil in a pan with the soy sauce and sugar. Add the vegetables and simmer 10 minutes. Let cool.

For the dressing, drop the tofu into a pan of boiling water, bring back to the boil, then drain. Place on a board, top with a plate and weight to squeeze out excess moisture. Force the tofu through a sieve into a bowl. Add the tahini, sugar and salt. Mix well. Drain the vegetables, reserving the liquid, and add them to the dressing with the ham, adding a little stock to thin if necessary. Serve cold.

▓ COOK'S TIP

An elegant dish, vegetarians can use vegetable instead of chicken stock, omit the ham and add a second type of mushroom, such as oyster mushrooms, for an interesting variation. The use of bean curd ensures the nutritional value of this recipe.

193 WHITE-COOKED CABBAGE

Preparation time:	YOU WILL NEED:
5 minutes, plus soaking	1 tablespoon dried shrimps
	1 Savoy or Chinese cabbage
	300 ml/ ½ pint Chinese stock (see
Cooking time:	recipe 2)
about 20 minutes	1 chicken stock cube
	25 g/1 oz lard
Serves 4	1 teaspoon sugar
	salt and pepper
Calories:	1½ tablespoons cooked chopped pork
150 per portion	or ham

Soak the dried shrimps in hot water for 10 minutes, then drain.

Remove the tough central stem from the cabbage, quarter it lengthways and cut each section in half. Bring the stock to the boil in a wok or saucepan. Stir in the stock cube, lard, shrimps and sugar. Simmer, stirring, for 2-3 minutes.

Add the cabbage to the pan, turning the pieces to ensure they are coated with the sauce. Bring to the boil, reduce the heat and simmer for 4 minutes. Toss the cabbage in the sauce, cover and simmer gently for a further 8-12 minutes.

Transfer the cabbage to a serving dish using a slotted spoon. Season the sauce with salt and pepper to taste and pour over the cabbage. Sprinkle with the pork or ham and serve hot.

194 STIR-FRIED SPICED CUCUMBER

Preparation time:	YOU WILL NEED:
5 minutes, plus salting	1½ cucumbers
	2 teaspoons salt
	1 tablespoon sunflower oil
Cooking time:	¼ teaspoon chilli bean sauce or
5 minutes	chilli powder
	6 garlic cloves, crushed
Serves 4	1½ tablespoons salted black beans,
	coarsely chopped
Calories:	5 tablespoons chicken stock
90 per portion	1 teaspoon sesame oil
	cucumber slices, to garnish

Peel the cucumbers and slice them in half lengthways. Remove the seeds and cut the flesh into cubes. Sprinkle with salt and leave to drain in a colander for 20 minutes. Rinse, drain and dry.

Heat the oil in a wok or frying pan and when it is almost smoking, add the chilli bean sauce or powder, garlic and black beans and stir-fry for 30 seconds. Add the cucumber and toss well for about 3 seconds to coat in the spices. Add the stock and continue stir-frying over a high heat for 3-4 minutes until almost all the liquid has evaporated and the cucumber is tender.

Transfer to a warmed serving dish, sprinkle with the sesame oil and garnish with cucumber slices. Serve at once.

▒ COOK'S TIP

Vegetables form a very important part of the Chinese diet, and cooking methods have been devised to make the most of their freshness and colour. White-cooking is a form of cooking in sauce that is particularly appropriate to leafy vegetables.

▒ COOK'S TIP

Cucumbers have been valued for their cooling properties since ancient times. They are refreshing even when cooked. Try this recipe with baked fish.

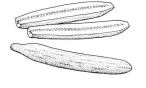

195 MIXED VEGETABLE SALAD WITH CHINESE DRESSING

Preparation time:
10 minutes

Serves 4-6

Calories:
91-61 per portion

YOU WILL NEED:
½ head Chinese leaves, or 1 celery heart
1 green pepper, cored and seeded
1 red pepper, cored and seeded
FOR THE DRESSING
1 teapoon salt
1 teaspoon sugar
4 tablespoons light soy sauce
2 tablespoons sesame oil

Remove and discard any tough outer parts of the Chinese leaves, then cut the head into thick slices. (If using celery, separate the sticks, then cut each one into thick slices.) Cut the green and red peppers diagonally into thin slices.

Place the Chinese leaves or celery in a bowl and arrange the red and green pepper on top. Sprinkle the salt and sugar evenly over the salad; leave to stand for a few minutes. Just before serving, sprinkle over the soy sauce and sesame seed oil and toss well.

196 STIR-FRIED BEANSPROUTS AND GREEN BEANS

Preparation time:
10 minutes

Cooking time:
2 minutes

Serves 4

Calories:
131 per portion

YOU WILL NEED:
450 g/1 lb fresh bean sprouts
225 g/8 oz dwarf French beans
3-4 tablespoons sunflower oil
1 spring onion, finely chopped
1 teaspoon salt
1 teaspoon sugar
1 teaspoon sesame oil

Wash and rinse the beansprouts in a basin of cold water, discarding the husks and other particles that float to the surface. Drain well. Top, tail and halve the French beans.

Heat the oil in a wok until it is smoking. Add the spring onion to flavour the oil, then add the beans and stir a few times.

Add the bean sprouts and stir-fry for 30 seconds. Add the salt and sugar and stir-fry for 1 minute more.

Serve hot, sprinkled with sesame oil.

▓ COOK'S TIP

Here is an exception to the usual Chinese form of 'salad', which is generally based on lightly cooked vegetables. Serve it with Shanghai spring rolls (recipe 220).

▓ COOK'S TIP

For this light and pretty Chinese dish, only fresh beansprouts should be used. Buy them on the day you plan to use them. Canned bean sprouts do not have the necessary crunchy texture to use them in this recipe.

197 PICKLED SALAD

Preparation time:	YOU WILL NEED:
15 minutes, plus standing	450 g/1 lb cucumber, peeled
	450 g/1 lb cabbage, cored and chopped
	2 teaspoons salt
Serves 4-6	1 teaspoon crushed garlic
	1 teaspoon ground Szechuan or
Calories:	black peppercorns
100-65 per portion	1 teaspoon sugar
	1 tablespoon light soy sauce
	2 tablespoons sesame oil
	1 tablespoon red wine vinegar

Crush the cucumbers until cracks appear on the surface. Quarter lengthways, then cut into pieces. Place in a bowl with the cabbage, sprinkle with salt and leave for 2 hours.

Rinse the vegetables and drain on absorbent kitchen paper. Mix together the garlic, pepper, sugar, soy sauce, oil and vinegar. Pour over the vegetables, mix well and allow to stand for at least 3 hours before serving. The salad looks attractive served on a cabbage-lined plate.

198 SPINACH SALAD WITH COCKLES AND MUSTARD SAUCE

Preparation time:	YOU WILL NEED:
15 minutes	1 tablespoon rice wine or dry sherry
	225 g/8 oz cockles, cleaned
Cooking time:	3 tablespoons soy sauce, plus
about 5 minutes	1 teaspoon
	1 teaspoon hot mustard
Serves 4	450 g/1 lb tender young spinach leaves,
	washed and trimmed
Calories:	salt
100 per portion	1 tablespoon sesame seeds, to garnish

Heat the rice wine or sherry in a small saucepan. Add the cockles and heat through. Drain, reserving the liquid.

In a bowl, mix 3 tablespoons of the soy sauce with the mustard. Add the cockles. Blanch the spinach leaves in lightly salted boiling water for 30 seconds, then drain and immediately plunge the leaves into a bowl of ice-cold water. Drain again and squeeze out any excess water. Pour over 1 teaspoon soy sauce.

Add the reserved liquid to the cockle mixture. Arrange the spinach on a serving plate. Place the cockle mixture in the centre and garnish with sesame seeds. Serve at once.

▨ COOK'S TIP

Salting the cucumber, to extract indigestible juices, is advisable in this recipe so that the texture is as crisp as possible.

▨ COOK'S TIP

This sharp, refreshing salad makes an excellent, unusual starter. Use only tender young spinach leaves, or use sorrel or rocket if available. Garnish it with a few radish flowers (see Cook's Tip 77), if liked.

199 BRAISED BEAN CURD

Preparation time:	YOU WILL NEED:
10 minutes, plus cooling	450 g/1 lb firm bean curd
	300ml/ ½ pint vegetable stock
	2 spring onions, trimmed
Cooking time:	1 x 5 cm/2 inch piece fresh root ginger,
40 minutes	peeled
	3 tablespoons light soy sauce
Serves 4	2 tablespoons Chinese wine or
	dry sherry
Calories:	1 tablespoon sugar
223 per portion	FOR THE GARNISH
	shredded spring onions
	carrot flowers (see recipe 123)

Put the bean curd in a saucepan, cover with cold water and bring to the boil. Cover the pan and cook over high heat for 10 minutes.

Meanwhile, put the stock in a separate saucepan with the spring onions and ginger. Bring to the boil and simmer gently for 5 minutes, to flavour the stock.

Drain the bean curd and add to the stock with the soy sauce, wine or sherry and sugar. Bring back to the boil, cover and simmer for 30 minutes. Turn off the heat and leave the bean curd to cool in the cooking liquid. Remove the bean curd from the pan with a slotted spoon and cut into slices. Arrange on a serving plate and serve garnished with spring onions and carrot flowers.

200 CRISPY BEAN CURD WITH TOMATO SAUCE

Preparation time:	YOU WILL NEED:
15 minutes	oil for deep-frying
	6 pieces bean curd, halved then cut into
Cooking time:	small triangles
40-45 minutes	3 large tomatoes, skinned, seeded
	and finely chopped
Serves 4	150 ml/ ¼ pint chicken stock
	1 tablespoon nam pla (fish sauce)
Calories:	pinch of salt
124 per portion	⅓ teaspoon sugar
	2 spring onion tops, cut into fine strips

Heat the oil in a wok or deep fat frier, add the bean curd and fry until it is golden brown. Remove from the oil with a slotted spoon and set aside.

Place the tomatoes in a medium saucepan with the chicken stock, nam pla, salt and sugar. Bring to the boil, reduce the heat and simmer for 15-20 minutes.

Add the bean curd and simmer for a further 10-15 minutes. The sauce should be thick and tasty. Serve immediately, with strips of spring onion arranged on top.

▨ COOK'S TIP

Bean curd is a valuable food, providing protein, oil, roughage, vitamins and salt. After cooking, the texture is like a honeycomb, and a crunchy garnish is essential.

▨ COOK'S TIP

The use of tomatoes is unusual in Oriental cookery. This recipe owes its origins to Vietnamese cuisine, which in turn is marked by French influences. Try to find a tomato variety grown for flavour rather than mere firmness and uniformity of size.

RICE & NOODLES

Because rice is the staple food of most Asian countries, it is looked upon as a precious commodity and is the basis of numerous wonderful main dishes and accompaniments. In wheat-growing northern China, noodles predominate, and they are featured in some irresistible recipes in this chapter.

201 TOMATO RICE

Preparation time:
5 minutes, plus soaking

Cooking time:
20-25 minutes

Serves 4

Calories:
320 per portion

YOU WILL NEED:
225 g/8 oz long-grain rice
3 tablespoons sunflower oil
1 onion, sliced
1 garlic clove, crushed
1 x 2.5 cm/1 inch piece fresh root ginger, peeled and chopped
1 x 539 g/1 lb 3 oz can tomatoes
salt
2 tablespoons finely chopped fresh coriander leaves

Wash the rice thoroughly under cold running water, then soak in cold water for 30 minutes; drain.

Heat the oil in a large pan, add the onion and fry until golden. Add the garlic and ginger and fry for 2 minutes. Add the rice, stir well and fry for 2 minutes, stirring to coat the grains with oil.

Break up the tomatoes in their juice and add to the rice with salt to taste. Bring to the boil, then cover and simmer for 15-20 minutes, until tender.

Transfer to a warmed serving dish and sprinkle with chopped coriander. Serve hot.

202 FRIED RICE

Preparation time:
25 minutes

Cooking time:
25 minutes

Serves 4-6

Calories:
433-289 per portion

YOU WILL NEED:
4 tablespoons sunflower oil
225 g/8 oz long-grain rice
3 garlic cloves, thinly sliced
2 teaspoons chopped fresh root ginger
6 spring onions, chopped
about 300 ml/ ½ pint chicken stock
100 g/4 oz button mushrooms, sliced
50 g/2 oz cooked ham, diced
50 g/2 oz peeled prawns
2 tablespoons light soy sauce
50 g/2 oz frozen peas
1 tablespoon freshly chopped coriander leaves

Heat the oil in a wok, add the rice and cook for about 5 minutes, until pale golden. Add the garlic, ginger and spring onions and stir well. Pour over sufficient boiling chicken stock just to cover the rice, bring to the boil, then cover and simmer for 20 minutes, stirring occasionally.

Fold in the mushrooms and cook for 2 minutes. Add the remaining ingredients and mix well. Cook for a further 5 minutes, stirring occasionally.

Pile into a warmed serving dish and serve immediately.

COOK'S TIP

The appeal of this flavourful dish is its colour. It makes an excellent accompaniment to fish, especially steamed whole fish, or can be served as a light meal on its own.

COOK'S TIP

Rice forms the staple diet for both China and India. Long-grain rice is the most popular variety in southern China; use it for all savoury dishes. Do not use 'easy cook' or *pre-cooked varieties as these lack the flavour, texture and colour which is essential to Oriental cuisine.*

203 YANGCHOW FRIED RICE

Preparation time:
25 minutes, plus
soaking

Cooking time:
10 minutes

Serves 4

Calories:
500 per portion

YOU WILL NEED:
175-225 g/6-8 oz long-grain rice
3-4 dried shiitake mushrooms
50 g/2 oz bamboo shoots
50 g/2 oz green peas
100 g/4 oz peeled prawns
100 g/4 oz cooked ham or pork
2-3 eggs
1 teaspoon salt
2 spring onions, finely chopped
3 tablespoons sunflower oil
1 ½ tablespoons light soy sauce

Prepare the rice as for Plain boiled rice (see recipe 206), and allow it to become quite cold. Soak the mushrooms in boiling water for 20 minutes. Drain, discard the hard stalks and dice the caps. Cut the bamboo shoots into equally small cubes. Cut the prawns into 2-3 pieces if large; dice the ham or pork.

Beat the eggs lightly with a pinch of the salt and about half of the spring onions. Heat 1 tablespoon of the oil in a wok or frying pan and scramble the eggs. Remove from the pan and set aside.

In a clean wok, heat the remaining oil and stir-fry the vegetables with the prawns and ham or pork. Add the cooked rice with the remaining salt and soy sauce, stirring to separate each grain of rice. Finally add the scrambled eggs, breaking them into small pieces. Add the remaining spring onions as a garnish and serve hot.

204 VEGETABLE RICE

Preparation time:
10 minutes

Cooking time:
15-20 minutes

Serves 4-6

Calories:
280-190 per portion

YOU WILL NEED:
2 tablespoons sunflower oil
2 leeks, washed and sliced
*1 x 1 cm/ ½ inch slice fresh root ginger,
    peeled and finely chopped*
1 garlic clove, thinly sliced
225 g/8 oz long-grain rice
salt
225 g/8 oz spring greens, shredded

Heat the oil in a wok or deep frying pan. Add the leeks, ginger and garlic and fry briskly for 30 seconds. Add the rice, stirring to coat each grain with the oil. Add sufficient boiling water to just cover the rice. Season to taste with salt. Bring to the boil, cover and simmer for 5 minutes.

Add the spring greens, bring back to the boil and simmer for 7-9 minutes until the rice is tender. Drain and serve at once.

▓ COOK'S TIP

This popular dish must have originated from the river port of the same name on the Yangtse Delta, but it is now on the menu of almost every Cantonese restaurant. You can vary the ingredients as you wish, substituting cooked pork for the ham, for example, carrots for the bamboo shoots and cubed green pepper for the peas.

▓ COOK'S TIP

To clean leeks, make a lengthways cut halfway down to the white part of the trimmed leek and hold the leaves open under running water to rinse away any soil.

205 CANTONESE RICE

Preparation time:	YOU WILL NEED:
30 minutes	225 g/8 oz long-grain rice, cooked
	100 g/4 oz prawns
Cooking time:	2 teaspoons salt
15 minutes	1 egg white, lightly beaten
	2 tablespoons cornflour
Serves 4	1 pig's kidney, halved and trimmed
	1 chicken liver, finely sliced
Calories:	100 g/4 oz green beans, halved
256 per portion	3 tablespoons sunflower oil
	2 spring onions, cut into short lengths
	100 g/4 oz roast pork, finely sliced
	100 g/4 oz white fish fillet, cubed
	1 teaspoon sugar
	2 tablespoons light soy sauce
	4 tablespoons Chinese stock (see recipe 2)

Cook the rice as for Plain boiled rice (see recipe 206) and keep hot. Put the prawns in a bowl with a pinch of salt, the egg white and 1 tablespoon of cornflour and toss to coat. Score the surface of each kidney half in a criss-cross pattern, then cut each half into 6-8 pieces. Blanch the prawns, kidney, liver and greens in boiling water for 10-15 seconds, and drain.

Heat the oil in a wok or pan and stir-fry the spring onions briefly. Add all the meats, fish and vegetables, with salt to taste, the sugar and soy sauce. Stir-fry for 1 minute. Combine the remaining cornflour with the stock and add to the wok, stirring. Serve on a bed of rice.

206 PLAIN BOILED RICE

Preparation time:	YOU WILL NEED:
5 minutes, plus	350 g/12 oz long-grain rice
soaking	450 ml/ ¾ pint water
	salt
Cooking time:	
20-25 minutes	
Serves 4	
Calories:	
300 per portion	

Wash the rice thoroughly under cold running water, then soak in cold water for 30 minutes. Drain.

Place the rice in a pan with the water and salt to taste. Bring to the boil, cover and simmer very gently for 20-25 minutes, until the rice in tender and the liquid absorbed. If cooking on an electric hob, the heat can be turned off once the rice has come to the boil.

Transfer the rice to a warmed serving dish. Serve as an accompaniment to spicy dishes or as the basis for savoury rice recipes.

▨ COOK'S TIP

This is a very popular dish served in Cantonese restaurants, known as Mixed meats or Assorted meats with rice. The ingredients vary enormously according to the chef's whims or seasonal availabilities. This recipe is only a suggestion — you may add or substitute as you like, or use any convenient leftovers.

▨ COOK'S TIP

Cooked rice will keep hot for up to 30 minutes in the sauce-pan. Cover it with a cloth to absorb any steam and prevent the grains from sticking together. Put the lid on top.

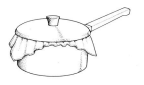

207 FRIED RICE WITH HAM AND BEANSPROUTS

Preparation time:
15 minutes

Cooking time:
8-10 minutes

Serves 4

Calories:
280 per portion

YOU WILL NEED:
2 tablespoons sunflower oil
2 spring onions, finely chopped
1 garlic clove, crushed
350 g/12 oz cooked long-grain rice
   (see recipe 206)
175 g/6 oz cooked ham, diced
2 tablespoons light soy sauce
2 eggs
salt and pepper
225 g/8 oz beansprouts, rinsed
   and drained

Heat the oil in a wok or pan over moderate heat and stir-fry the spring onions and garlic for 2 minutes. Add the rice and stir well. Cook gently, stirring as the rice heats through.

Stir in the ham and soy sauce. Beat the eggs with salt and pepper to taste. Pour into the rice mixture in a thin stream, stirring all the time. Add the beansprouts and continue cooking, stirring until all the ingredients are hot and the eggs are set. Serve at once.

208 SPICY FRIED RICE

Preparation time:
15 minutes, plus
soaking

Cooking time:
about 40 minutes

Serves 4

Calories:
420 per portion

YOU WILL NEED:
350 g/12 oz long-grain rice
450 ml/ ¾ pint water
salt
2 tablespoons sunflower oil
4 shallots or 1 onion, thinly sliced
2 fresh red chillies, seeded and
   thinly sliced
50 g/2 oz chopped pork, beef or bacon
1 tablespoon light soy sauce
1 teaspoon tomato purée
FOR THE GARNISH
a few slices of fried onion
1 plain omelette, made with 1 egg,
   cut into strips
a few fresh coriander leaves
a few cucumber slices

Prepare and cook the rice as for Plain boiled rice (see recipe 206).

Heat the oil in a wok or frying pan, add the shallots and chillies and fry for 1-3 minutes. Add the meat or bacon and fry for 3 minutes, stirring constantly. Add the rice, soy sauce and tomato purée and stir-fry for 5-8 minutes, then season with salt to taste.

Transfer to a warmed serving dish and garnish with the onion, omelette, coriander and cucumber. Serve at once.

▨ COOK'S TIP

An ideal supper dish with a salad, all the ingredients for this rice recipe can be prepared in advance and stir-fried together just before serving.

▨ COOK'S TIP

Incorporating carbohydrate, protein and vitamins, this savoury dish is a meal on its own. In China and South-East Asia, however, it is often served with baked or grilled fish. If you find the chillies make it too hot, use paprika pepper instead and the colour will be just as attractive.

209 NOODLES TOSSED WITH MEAT AND VEGETABLES

Preparation time:
20 minutes

Cooking time:
about 5 minutes

Serves 4-6

Calories:
550-360 per portion

YOU WILL NEED:
2 carrots, peeled
3 celery sticks
½ cucumber
2 fresh green chillies, seeded
2 tablespoons oil
1 garlic clove, chopped
350 g/12 oz minced pork
4 spring onions, sliced
1 small green pepper, cored, seeded
    and sliced
1 tablespoon light soy sauce
2 tablespoons red bean paste
1 tablespoon Chinese wine or
    dry sherry
350 g/12 oz noodles, cooked

Cut the carrots, celery and cucumber into matchstick lengths. Slice the chillies finely.

Heat the oil in a wok or deep frying pan. Add the chillies and garlic and fry briskly for 30 seconds. Add the pork and cook for 2 minutes. Increase the heat, add the vegetables and cook for 1 minute. Stir in the soy sauce, red bean paste, wine or sherry and the noodles. Stir well to combine the ingredients and heat through.

Pile on to a warmed serving dish and serve at once.

210 CRISPY FRIED NOODLES

Preparation time:
15 minutes

Cooking time:
about 15 minutes

Serves 4-6

Calories:
500-330 per portion

YOU WILL NEED:
3 celery sticks
100 g/4 oz spinach leaves
450 g/1 lb egg noodles
salt
1 tablespoon sunflower oil
1 garlic clove, sliced
1 x 5 cm/2 inch piece fresh root ginger,
    peeled and finely chopped
3 spring onions, chopped
100 g/4 oz lean pork, sliced
100 g/4 oz boneless chicken breast,
    shredded
1 tablespoon light soy sauce
1 tablespoon Chinese wine or
    dry sherry
50 g/2 oz peeled prawns

Slice the celery sticks diagonally. Wash the spinach leaves and cut into shreds.

Cook the noodles in boiling salted water until just tender. Drain and rinse with cold water.

Heat the oil in a wok or deep frying pan. Add the garlic, ginger and spring onions and stir-fry for 1 minute. Add the pork and chicken and stir-fry for 2 minutes. Add the noodles, soy sauce, wine or sherry and prawns and cook for 3 minutes, still stirring.

Pile on to a warmed serving dish and serve at once.

■ COOK'S TIP

The vegetables in this dish are cut into strips to complement the shape of the noodles. Toss the ingredients together well before serving.

■ COOK'S TIP

Noodles are the staple food of the wheat-growing northern provinces of China, known generally as mien, though there are several different varieties. This dish has a relatively large proportion of meat, but you can leave out either the pork or the chicken if you wish, perhaps substituting straw or button mushrooms.

211 LOTUS LEAF RICE

Preparation time:
20 minutes, plus
soaking

Cooking time:
25 minutes

Serves 4-6

Calories:
261-174 per portion

YOU WILL NEED:
8 lotus leaves
1 tablespoon sunflower oil
1 garlic clove, crushed
3 spring onions, chopped
100 g/4 oz button mushrooms, sliced
50 g/2 oz cooked ham, diced
100 g/4 oz cooked chicken, diced
1 tablespoon green peas
50 g/ 2oz canned bamboo shoots,
    drained and chopped
175 g/6 oz long-grain rice, cooked (see
    recipe 206)
2 tablespoons light soy sauce
2 tablespoons Chinese wine or
    dry sherry

Soak the lotus leaves in warm water for 30 minutes. Drain thoroughly.

Heat the oil in a wok or deep frying pan, add the garlic and spring onions and stir-fry for 1 minute. Add the remaining ingredients, except the lotus leaves, and cook for 2 minutes.

Cut each lotus leaf into 2 or 3 pieces and divide the mixture among them. Fold the leaf sections to enclose the filling like a parcel, and secure with string. Place in a steamer and steam vigorously for 15-20 minutes.

Pile the parcels on to a warmed serving dish and serve immediately. Each diner opens his own parcels.

212 TRANSPARENT NOODLES WITH PORK

Preparation time:
10 minutes, plus
soaking

Cooking time:
4-5 minutes

Serves 4

Calories:
224 per portion

YOU WILL NEED:
100 g/4 oz transparent noodles
225 g/8 oz lean minced pork
1 teaspoon cornflour
2 tablespoons light soy sauce
1 tablespoon hot black bean paste
100 ml/ 4 fl oz chicken stock or water
4 tablespoons sunflower oil
4 spring onions, finely chopped
1 fresh green chilli, seeded and
    finely chopped

Soak the noodles in warm water for 10 minutes. Drain. Mix the pork with the cornflour and soy sauce. Combine the bean paste with the stock or water.

Heat the oil in a wok or large frying pan over high heat. Add the pork and stir-fry for about 2 minutes until it has browned. Stir in the noodles, spring onions, chilli and finally the bean paste mixture. Bring to the boil and stir for about 1 minute, until all the moisture has evaporated. Transfer to a warmed serving dish and serve immediately.

▨ COOK'S TIP

Dried lotus leaves are used for wrapping food, but when fresh they can add a distinct flavour to dishes. If you can't buy them, use one vine leaf for each parcel instead.

▨ COOK'S TIP

Beanthread, cellophane or transparent noodles, as they are variously called, are usually used in soups and stews in Chinese cooking. Here they are used to add bulk to a savoury stir-fry which makes a delicious and filling all-in-one dish.

213 SINGAPORE NOODLES

Preparation time:	YOU WILL NEED:
15 minutes	2 nests dry noodles
	500 ml/18 fl oz water
Cooking time:	100 g/4 oz lean pork, cut into
17 minutes	5 cm/2 inch strips
	75 g/3 oz uncooked shelled prawns
Serves 4	75 g/3 oz squid, cleaned and sliced
	(see recipe 7)
Calories:	4 tablespoons sunflower oil
195 per portion	2 garlic cloves, crushed
	75 g/3 oz beansprouts
	1 tablespoon light soy sauce
	1 tablespoon dark soy sauce
	½ teaspoon freshly ground black pepper
	1 bunch fresh chives, chopped
	2 eggs

Boil the noodles in plenty of water for 2 minutes. Drain. Bring the measured water to the boil in a pan and cook the pork, prawns and squid together for 5 minutes. Drain and reserve the liquid.

Heat the oil in a wok or frying pan and fry the garlic until golden. Add the beansprouts and noodles, increase the heat, and stir-fry for 2 minutes. Add the pork, prawns and squid, the soy sauces, pepper and chives and stir-fry for 1 minute more.

Push the mixture to one side of the pan and crack in the eggs. Cook for 1 minute and add the reserved liquid. Bring to the boil and cook for 2 minutes, stirring well. Transfer to a warmed serving dish and serve at once.

▓ COOK'S TIP

The original version of this dish is a rich mixture of noodles, beansprouts, pork, squid, prawns, egg and rich meat stock, though it can be modified to suit your taste.

214 DAN-DAN NOODLES

Preparation time:	YOU WILL NEED:
15 minutes	450 g/1 lb noodles
	salt
Cooking time:	2 tablespoons tahini (sesame
about 20 minutes	seed paste)
	6 spring onions, chopped
Serves 4	2 garlic cloves, crushed
	1 × 5 cm/2 inch piece root ginger,
Calories:	peeled and finely chopped
500 per portion	1 tablespoon light soy sauce
	2 teaspoons red wine vinegar
	900 ml/1½ pints beef or chicken stock
	2 teaspoons hot pepper oil (optional)

Cook the noodles in boiling salted water until just tender. Drain and keep hot.

Blend the tahini with 4 tablespoons water and place in a pan with the spring onions, garlic, ginger, soy sauce and vinegar. Cook over a moderate heat, stirring frequently, for about 5 minutes.

Meanwhile, bring the stock to the boil in a pan and simmer for 2 minutes. Divide the noodles and hot sauce between 4 individual soup bowls. Spoon over the hot stock and top with the hot pepper oil, if using. Serve at once.

▓ COOK'S TIP

This is a delicious and nourishing dish for vegetarians. The rich sauce is best offset with refreshing vegetables for an accompaniment, such as Stir-fried beansprouts (recipe 196) or Celery salad (recipe 173).

215 MIXED SEAFOOD STICK NOODLES

Preparation time: about 15 minutes, plus soaking	**YOU WILL NEED:** 4 dried shiitake mushrooms 450 g/1 lb rice stick noodles salt
Cooking time: about 15 minutes	2 tablespoons sunflower oil 4 spring onions, chopped 2 garlic cloves, sliced
Serves 4-6	1 x 5 cm/2 inch piece fresh root ginger, peeled and finely chopped 50 g/2 oz peeled prawns
Calories: 550-360 per portion	100 g/4 oz squid, sliced (optional) 1 x 225 g/7 ½ oz can clams, drained 2 tablespoons Chinese wine or dry sherry 1 tablespoon light soy sauce

Soak the mushrooms in boiling water for 20 minutes. Drain, discard the hard stalks and slice the caps.

Cook the noodles in boiling salted water for 7-8 minutes until just tender. Drain, rinse in cold water, and set aside.

Heat the oil in a wok or deep frying pan and stir-fry the spring onions, garlic and ginger for 30 seconds. Stir in the mushrooms, prawns and squid, if using, and cook for 2 minutes. Stir in the remaining ingredients and the noodles and heat through. Pour into a warmed serving dish and serve at once.

216 SOFT NOODLES WITH CRAB MEAT SAUCE

Preparation time: 15-20 minutes	**YOU WILL NEED:** 150 g/5 oz egg noodles pinch of salt
Cooking time: 10 minutes	2 tablespoons sunflower oil 1 x 112 g/4 oz can crab meat, drained 100 g/4 oz spinach, rinsed and cut into rough pieces
Serves 2-3	1 teaspoon light soy sauce
Calories: 338-226 per portion	250 ml/8 fl oz Chinese stock (see recipe 2) 1 spring onion, finely chopped, to garnish

Cook the noodles in plenty of boiling salted water until they are just tender. Drain and keep warm.

Heat the oil in a wok or deep frying pan over moderate heat. Stir-fry the crab meat and spinach for 2 minutes. Add the soy sauce and stock and cook, stirring, for 2-3 minutes.

Arrange the noodles in a warmed serving dish and pour the sauce over. Garnish with chopped spring onion and serve at once.

▦ COOK'S TIP

The seafood ingredients here can be varied according to taste. Try scallops and mussels and garnish with diced red or green pepper for extra vitamins and colour.

▦ COOK'S TIP

Pink, white and green, this pretty dish appeals to the Chinese ideal of food that looks as appetizing as it tastes. To keep the colours fresh and bright, the cooking time should be minimal.

SIDE DISHES

In a typical Chinese meal many dishes are presented at once, some light, some substantial, each prepared by a different method. Side dishes make up an indispensable element in such a feast, from savoury Pork and spring onion pancakes to the refreshing tartness of Sweet and sour cucumber and Festive vegetable achar.

217 SHANGHAI SPRING ROLLS

Preparation time:
15-20 minutes, plus marinating

Cooking time:
about 20 minutes

Makes about 20

Calories:
45 per roll

YOU WILL NEED:
1 pack (20) ready-made frozen spring
   roll skins, thawed
225 g/8 oz pork fillet, finely shredded
1 tablespoon light soy sauce
1 tablespoon Chinese wine
2 teaspoons cornflour
5-6 dried shiitake mushrooms
oil for deep-frying
100 g/4 oz bamboo shoots, shredded
225 g/8 oz young leeks, shredded
1 teaspoon salt
1 teaspoon sugar
flour for dredging

Cover the spring roll skins with a damp cloth to prevent them drying out. For the filling, marinate the pork in the soy sauce, wine and cornflour 30 minutes. Soak the mushrooms in boiling water 20 minutes. Drain, discard the stalks and shred the caps.

Heat 3 tablespoons of oil in a wok and stir-fry the pork until it takes colour. Add the mushrooms, bamboo shoots and leeks. Stir-fry briefly then add the salt and sugar. Cook for 2 minutes, remove the mixture and leave to cool.

To make the spring rolls, shape 1 tablespoon of filling into a 7.5 cm/3 inch sausage shape and place it about a third of the way down on a spring roll skin. Fold up as shown in Cook's Tip, brushing the open flap with a flour and water paste to seal and make a neat package. Repeat with the remaining skins. Deep-fry the rolls in hot oil for 3-4 minutes in batches of 5 or 6 until crisp and golden.

COOK'S TIP

After they have been prepared, the spring rolls can be kept in the refrigerator for a day or frozen for up to 3 months.

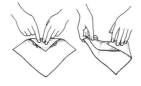

218 CRISPY PANCAKE ROLLS

Preparation time:
10 minutes

Cooking time:
45 minutes

Serves 4-6

Calories:
350-230 per portion

YOU WILL NEED:
225 g/8 oz plain flour
pinch of salt
1 egg
about 300 ml/ ½ pint water
oil for deep-frying
FOR THE FILLING
1 tablespoon sunflower oil
1 teaspoon chopped fresh root ginger
2 garlic cloves, crushed
225 g/8 oz boneless chicken breast,
   skinned and diced
2 tablespoons light soy sauce
1 tablespoon Chinese wine
100 g/4 oz mushrooms, sliced
3 spring onions, chopped
50 g/ 2oz peeled prawns

Sift the flour and salt into a bowl, add the egg and beat in enough water to make a smooth batter. Use to make thin pancakes in a 20 cm/8 inch frying pan.

Heat the oil in a wok or frying pan and stir-fry the ginger and garlic for 30 seconds. Add the chicken and brown quickly. Stir in the soy sauce and wine, then the mushrooms and spring onions. Increase the heat and cook for 1 minute. Remove from the heat, stir in the prawns and cool.

Place 2-3 tablespoons of the filling in the centre of each pancake. Fold in the sides and form into a tight roll, sealing the edge with a little flour and water paste. Deep-fry the rolls a few at a time for 2-3 minutes. Drain and serve hot.

COOK'S TIP

Pancake rolls are a popular starter or snack, but they make luxurious accompaniments to composite rice dishes or a whole baked or steamed fish.

Chinese menus should include dishes prepared by different methods — these savouries have a tempting crispness that goes well with boiled or steamed foods.

219 PORK AND SPRING ONION PANCAKES

Preparation time:
20 minutes

Cooking time:
30 minutes

Makes 24

Calories:
105 per portion

YOU WILL NEED:
1 × recipe pancake dough (see recipe 220)
100 g/4 oz cooked pork, finely chopped
6 spring onions, finely chopped
1 tablespoon salt
2 tablespoons Chinese wine or dry sherry
1 tablespoon sesame oil
oil for shallow frying

Divide the dough in 24 pieces and shape each one into a long, flat oval (see Cook's Tip).

Mix the pork and onions with the salt, wine or sherry and sesame oil. Scatter about 1 tablespoon of the filling over each pancake. Fold in the 2 long sides to the centre, over the filling, and then fold each pancake in half lengthways. Form into a round, flat coil and tuck in the ends. Roll the coil flat.

Shallow fry each pancake for about 5 minutes over a moderate heat, turning once to brown both sides. Serve hot.

220 MANDARIN PANCAKES

Preparation time:
20 minutes

Cooking time:
about 15-20 minutes

Makes 24

Calories:
160 per 2 pancakes

YOU WILL NEED:
450 g/1 lb plain flour
300 ml/ ½ pint boiling water
1 teaspoon salt
sunflower oil

Sift the flour into a bowl. Mix the water with the salt and gradually stir it into the flour. Mix to make a firm dough. Divide the dough into 24 pieces and press each into a flat pancake with the palm of your hand. Brush one pancake with a little oil, then top with a second to make a 'sandwich'. Repeat to make a total of 12 'sandwiches'. Roll out each to make a 15 cm/6 inch circle.

Heat an ungreased frying pan over a moderate heat and, when it is hot, fry the 'sandwiches' one at a time until bubbles appear on the surface. Turn over and cook until the underside has brown spots. Remove from the pan and peel the pancakes apart for serving. Fold into quarters and arrange on a warmed serving platter.

■ COOK'S TIP

A savoury filling makes the pancakes special for a party. Vary the ingredients with tiny shrimps, finely diced peppers, a hint of chilli or slivers of celery.

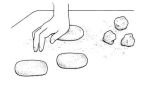

■ COOK'S TIP

Mandarin pancakes are an indispensable accompaniment to Peking Duck (see recipe 104). After spreading with sauce, place a little of the meat and vegetables on the pancake, fold in the edges and roll it up. Use balanced quantities of each ingredient for the correct effect.

221 FESTIVE VEGETABLE ACHAR

Preparation time:
45 minutes, plus
chilling

Cooking time:
8 minutes

Serves 4

Calories:
351 per portion

YOU WILL NEED:
5 cabbage leaves
1 cucumber
3 carrots, trimmed
1 head cauliflower
1.5 litres/2½ pints vinegar
20 shallots, peeled and chopped
2 tablespoons shredded root ginger
1 thumb-size piece fresh turmeric
3 red chillies, seeded and chopped
2 teaspoons shrimp paste
5 macadamia nuts
1 large onion, chopped
6 tablespoons sunflower oil
200 g/7 oz peanuts
3 tablespoons sugar
4 tablespoons sesame seeds

Cut the cabbage, cucumber and carrots into narrow strips. Separate the cauliflower into florets.

Bring the vinegar to the boil in a saucepan and drop in handfuls of the cabbage, cucumber, carrots, cauliflower and shallots to scald for 1 minute. Lift out and drain well.

Work the ginger, turmeric, chillies, shrimp paste, macadamia nuts and onion to a thick paste. Heat the oil in a wok or frying pan and fry this mixture for 5 minutes. Place in a glass or enamel (not metal) bowl and mix in the vegetables thoroughly. Refrigerate for at least 1 day, preferably longer. To serve, mix in the peanuts and sugar and sprinkle the sesame seeds on top.

222 CRUNCHY PICKLED CUCUMBER

Preparation time:
10 minutes, plus
marinating

Makes about
450 g/1 lb

Total Calories:
143

YOU WILL NEED:
4 teaspoons salt
4 dried chillies, seeded and shredded
3 tablespoons gin
2 medium cucumbers, thinly sliced
600 ml/1 pint malt vinegar

Sprinkle the salt, chillies and gin over the cucumber slices in a shallow glass or ceramic dish. Leave for 2 hours for the flavours to blend.

Place the mixture in perfectly clean jars and pour in the vinegar to cover completely. Seal with clingfilm or a tight-fitting lid and leave to stand for 3 days before use, turning or shaking the jars once a day.

■ COOK'S TIP

This spicy pickle is prepared in great quantities for Chinese New Year. If you cannot obtain fresh turmeric or galangal, which is a close relative, you may omit it.

■ COOK'S TIP

Pickles are a regular accompaniment to rich fish or meat dishes in the cuisine of Szechuan. This recipe works equally well with cabbage. Use hard white cabbage and slice it very thinly. Cucumber is the most suitable partner for fish dishes, cabbage for those based on meat.

223 MUSTARD-PICKLED AUBERGINE

Preparation time:	YOU WILL NEED:
15 minutes, plus standing and chilling	1 medium aubergine, or 6 small long aubergines
	750 ml/1¼ pints water
Serves 4	1 tablespoon salt
	FOR THE DRESSING
Calories:	1 teaspoon mustard powder
73 per portion	3 tablespoons soy sauce
	3 tablespoons Chinese wine or medium dry sherry
	4 tablespoons sugar

Cut the aubergine in 3 mm/ ⅛ inch slices, and cut each slice into quarters. Soak in the water, with the salt added, for 1 hour.

To make the dressing, put all the ingredients in a bowl and stir well to combine.

Drain the aubergine slices and pat them dry with absorbent kitchen paper. Arrange them carefully in a glass or ceramic serving bowl and pour the dressing over evenly and slowly.

Cover the bowl with clingfilm and chill in the refrigerator for several hours or overnight before serving, to allow the flavours to marry.

Garnish with cucumber rings, if liked (see Cook's Tip).

224 SWEET AND SOUR CUCUMBER

Preparation time:	YOU WILL NEED:
25-30 minutes	1 cucumber
	1 teaspoon salt
Total Calories:	2 tablespoons caster sugar
136	2 tablespoons vinegar

Split the cucumber in half lengthways, then cut it into strips the size of large potato chips. Sprinkle over the salt and leave to stand for 10 minutes.

Drain off any excess liquid from the cucumber chips and arrange on a serving platter. Sprinkle first with sugar, then vinegar, and serve.

COOK'S TIP

To make cucumber rings, cut 5 mm/ ¼ inch slices from an unpeeled cucumber and remove the seeds. Make a cut in one ring and loop it through another.

COOK'S TIP

Select a dark green cucumber that is slender rather than fat and overgrown for this dish. The large, pale green ones contain too much water and have far less flavour.

DESSERTS

Few of the many sweets enjoyed in China are served in the West. Here is a representative selection of easily prepared desserts to end a Chinese meal in style. Fruit-based sweets such as Almond fruit salad predominate, as they are the perfect balance to a rich or salty meal. Eight-treasure rice pudding is a festive dish for special occasions, while desserts such as Sweet green pea cubes and Fruit fritters can be served at any time of day with a cup of China tea.

225 PEKING TOFFEE APPLES

Preparation time:	YOU WILL NEED:
15 minutes	100 g/4 oz plain flour
	1 egg
Cooking time:	100 ml/3½ fl oz water, plus
20 minutes	2 tablespoons
	4 crisp apples, peeled, cored and cut
Serves 4	into thick slices
	600 ml/1 pint sunflower oil, plus
Calories:	1 tablespoon
319 per portion	6 tablespoons sugar
	3 tablespoons golden syrup

Mix together the flour, egg and 100 ml/3½ fl oz of the water to make a smooth batter. Dip each piece of apple in the batter.

In a wok or deep frying pan heat 600 ml/1 pint of the oil to 180 C/350 F or until a cube of bread browns in 30 seconds. Deep-fry the apple pieces for 2 minutes, remove with a slotted spoon and drain on absorbent kitchen paper.

In a clean pan, heat together the sugar, the remaining oil and water. Dissolve the sugar over a gentle heat, then simmer for 5 minutes, stirring constantly. Add the golden syrup and and boil to the hard crack stage (151 C/304 F on a sugar thermometer), when the syrup forms brittle threads when dropped into iced water. Place the fried apples in the syrup and coat all over. Remove with a slotted spoon and drop into iced water. Remove immediately and serve, decorated with fresh apple slices if liked.

226 FRUIT FRITTERS

Preparation time:	YOU WILL NEED:
10 minutes	2 large, firm eating apples, peeled
	and cored
Cooking time:	2 bananas, halved lengthways
about 15 minutes	1 egg
	4 tablespoons cornflour
Serves 8	vegetable oil for deep-frying
	100 g/4 oz sugar
Calories:	3 tablespoons sesame oil
300 per portion	1 tablespoon sesame seeds
	FOR THE DECORATION
	lime slices
	banana slices

Cut each apple into 8 pieces. Cut each piece of banana into 3-4 pieces. Beat the egg, then blend in the cornflour and enough cold water to make a smooth batter.

Heat the oil in a wok or deep-frier to 180 C/350 F or until a cube of day old bread browns in 30 seconds. Dip each piece of fruit in the batter and deep-fry for 2-3 minutes. Drain on absorbent kitchen paper.

Heat the sugar and sesame oil in a pan over a low heat for 5 minutes. Add 3 tablespoons of water and stir for 2 minute. Add the fruit fritters and the sesame seeds and stir slowly, until each fritter is covered with syrup. As soon as the syrup has caramelized, remove the fritters and plunge them into a bowl of ice-cold water to harden the 'toffee'. Serve decorated with lime and banana slices.

▨ COOK'S TIP

Apple pieces encased in toffee make a delicious dessert. In Chinese restaurants they are brought to the table piping hot, and guests pick them up with chopsticks and dip them into a bowl of ice-cold water to set the caramel.

▨ COOK'S TIP

Fruit fritters are among the most popular Chinese desserts. Include them in a menu which does not depend heavily on deep-fried dishes.

227 RICE-STUFFED PEARS

Preparation time:	YOU WILL NEED:
10 minutes	225 g/8 oz flaked rice
	25 g/1 oz almonds, skinned
Cooking time:	and roughly chopped
40 minutes	1 x 100 g/4 oz can lotus seeds, drained
	and roughly chopped
Serves 4	6 red and green glacé cherries, finely
	chopped
Calories:	50 ml/2 fl oz sunflower oil
460 per portion	2 tablespoons sugar
	4 pears, peeled, halved and cored
	FOR THE SAUCE
	1 tablespoon sugar
	100 ml/3½ fl oz water
	25 g/1 oz cornflour
	1-2 drops pink food colouring
	(optional)

Place the flaked rice in a bowl, cover with water and steam for 30 minutes.

Mix together the cooked rice, almonds, lotus seeds, cherries, oil and sugar.

To make the sauce, dissolve the sugar in the water. Blend the cornflour with the food colouring (if using) and add this to the syrup. Bring to the boil.

Spoon the rice mixture into the pear halves and steam for about 15 minutes. Serve with the sauce poured over.

228 ALMOND FRUIT SALAD

Preparation time:	YOU WILL NEED:
15 minutes, plus	4 dessert apples, cored
chilling	4 peaches, skinned and stoned
	100 g/4 oz strawberries
Cooking time:	4 slices pineapple
10 minutes	100 g/4 oz lychees, skinned
	FOR THE ALMOND SYRUP
Serves 4-6	1 tablespoon cornflour
	450 ml/ ¾ pint plus 2 tablespoons water
Calories:	2 tablespoons ground almonds
250-170 per portion	3 tablespoons sugar

Make the syrup first. Blend the cornflour with 2 tablespoons of water and place in a pan with the ground almonds, remaining water and sugar. Gradually bring to the boil, stirring, then simmer for 10 minutes, stirring constantly. Remove from the heat and leave to cool, stirring occasionally to prevent a skin forming.

Slice the apples, peaches and strawberries. Cut the pineapple into cubes. Put all the fruit in a bowl and mix well. Spoon over the almond syrup and serve lightly chilled.

▨ COOK'S TIP

This delicate pink and white dessert is a pretty way to end a special meal. Vary the recipe by leaving the pears whole. Remove the cores and push the stuffing down the centre. Whole pears will take a few minutes longer to cook.

▨ COOK'S TIP

If preparing this salad in advance, sprinkle with lemon juice to prevent the apples discolouring. Other fruits for inclusion are nectarines, pears and bananas.

229 LYCHEE SORBET

Preparation time:
30 minutes, plus
chilling

Cooking time:
about 15 minutes

Serves 4

Calories:
196 per portion

YOU WILL NEED:
1 x 500 g/1 lb can lychees
100 g/4 oz granulated sugar
2 tablespoons lemon or lime juice
2 egg whites
thinly pared rind of 1 lime, to decorate

Drain the juice from the lychees into a jug and make up to 300 ml/ ½ pint with cold water. Place in a pan and add the sugar. Heat gently to dissolve the sugar, then bring to the boil. Simmer without stirring for 10 minutes. Remove from the heat and leave to cool slightly.

Purée the lychees in a blender or press through a sieve. Mix the purée with the sugar syrup and lemon or lime juice. Pour into a shallow freezer container and place in the freezer for 1-2 hours, or until almost frozen.

Whisk the egg whites until fairly stiff. Cut the frozen mixture into small pieces and work in a food processor to break down the crystals. Do not let the mixture melt; quickly incorporate the beaten egg white, then pour into a slightly deeper freezer container. Return to the freezer until firm.

Blanch the lime rind in boiling water for 2 minutes, drain and refresh in cold water. Cut into thin strips.

Ten minutes before serving, scoop the sorbet into individual glass dishes and decorate with lime rind.

230 BEAN AND KIWI FOOL

Preparation time:
10 minutes, plus
soaking and chilling

Cooking time:
45 minutes-1 hour

Serves 8

Calories:
260 per portion

YOU WILL NEED:
175 g/6 oz mung beans, soaked in
cold water overnight, drained
and rinsed
100 ml/ 4 fl oz milk
300 ml/ ½ pint double cream
1½ tablespoons brown sugar
2 tablespoons medium sherry
1 teaspoon vanilla flavouring
2 kiwi fruit, peeled and puréed,
to decorate

Place the beans in a large pan and cover with fresh cold water. Bring to the boil, half cover and cook for 45 minutes-1 hour until tender. Drain well.

Work the cooked beans to a purée in a food processor. Add the milk and 100 ml/4 fl oz of the cream and mix to a thick consistency. Add the sugar, sherry and vanilla flavouring. Pour into 8 individual glasses or bowls and chill for at least 2 hours.

To serve, pour a little of the kiwi fruit purée on top of each pudding. Whip the remaining cream until thick, then spoon or pipe on top. Serve well chilled.

▓ COOK'S TIP

The delicate flavour of this exotic fruit makes a most refreshing sorbet. Serve on its own or in partnership with crunchy-sweet Fruit fritters.

▓ COOK'S TIP

A rich and filling sweet, small quantities are enough to end an elegant meal. Cream is rarely used in Chinese cookery — this recipe is borrowed from Vietnam

where the French influence is strong.

231 SWEET GREEN PEA CUBES

Preparation time:
20 minutes, plus
soaking

Cooking time:
1 hour 15 minutes

Serves 4

Calories:
286 per portion

YOU WILL NEED:
225 g/8 oz green split peas
600 ml/1 pint water plus 4 tablespoons
75 g/3 oz sugar
2 tablespoons cornflour

Soak the peas in 600 ml/1 pint of water for 4 hours. Bring to the boil, cover and simmer for about 45 minutes until soft. Put the peas and any remaining liquid through a fine sieve. Return to a clean pan.

Stir in the sugar, and the cornflour blended with 4 tablespoons water. Bring the peas to the boil, stirring. Turn the heat to the lowest setting and cook, stirring, for 10 minutes. Pour the mixture into a lightly oiled shallow dish or freezing tray so it is about 2.5 cm/1 inch deep. Chill in the refrigerator for 1 hour or until very firm.

Cut the block into cubes and pile them up on a serving plate in a pyramid. To serve, spear the cubes from the plate using cocktail sticks.

232 RICE FRITTERS

Preparation time:
10 minutes

Cooking time:
about 5-10 minutes

Makes about 20

Calories:
100 per fritter

YOU WILL NEED:
160 g/5 ½ oz cooked medium grain rice
2 eggs, beaten
3 tablespoons sugar
½ teaspoon vanilla essence
50 g/2 oz plain flour
1 tablespoon baking powder
pinch of salt
25 g/1 oz desiccated coconut
vegetable oil for deep-frying
sifted icing sugar, for sprinkling

Put the rice, eggs, sugar and vanilla in a bowl and mix well. Sift together the flour, baking powder and salt, then stir into the rice mixture. Stir in the coconut.

Heat the oil in a deep fat frier to 180 C/350 F or until a cube of day-old bread browns in 30 seconds. Drop tablespoonfuls of the mixture into the hot oil, one at a time, and deep-fry until golden on all sides. Drain on absorbent kitchen paper.

Transfer to a warmed serving dish and sprinkle with a generous amount of icing sugar. Serve hot.

COOK'S TIP

These cubes of sweetened green pea purée are served in China as a sweetmeat to round off a late meal with friends. Serve with little cups of jasmine tea.

COOK'S TIP

Not surprisingly, a number of Chinese desserts are based on sweetened rice and many of them are essential features of the festive meals which punctuate the year. These sweet fritters, crunchy on the outside, are delectably soft within.

233 ALMOND FLOAT

Preparation time:
20 minutes, plus
settting

Cooking time:
20 minutes

Serves 4

Calories:
107 per portion

YOU WILL NEED:
15 g/ ½ oz agar-agar or isinglass, or
    25 g/1 oz powdered gelatine
4 tablespoons sugar
300 ml/ ½ pint milk
1 teaspoon almond flavouring
1 x 400 g/14 oz can apricots, or mixed
    fruit salad
50 g/2 oz white grapes, peeled
    and seeded

Dissolve the agar-agar or isinglass in 300 ml/½ pint water over gentle heat. (If using gelatine, dissolve in the water according to packet instructions.) Dissolve the sugar in 300 ml/ ½ pint water in a separate saucepan, then combine with the dissolved setting agent and add the milk and almond flavouring. Pour this mixture into a large serving bowl. Leave until cold, then chill in the refrigerator for at least 3 hours, until set.

To serve, cut the junket into small cubes and place in a serving bowl. Pour the canned fruit and syrup over the junket, add the grapes and mix well. Serve chilled.

234 WALNUT SWEET

Preparation time:
5 minutes, plus
soaking

Cooking time:
5-10 minutes

Serves 4-6

Calories:
500-350 per portion

YOU WILL NEED:
100 g/4 oz shelled walnuts
3 tablespoons sunflower oil
75 g/3 oz dates, stoned
900 ml/1 ½ pints water
150 g/5 oz sugar
40 g/1 ½ oz ground rice
3 tablespoons milk
apple flower, to decorate (see
    Cook's Tip)

Soak the walnuts in boiling water for 10 minutes, drain and remove the skins. Dry on absorbent kitchen paper.

Heat the oil in a wok or deep frying pan. Add the walnuts and fry quickly until lightly browned (take care not to burn them). Drain on absorbent kitchen paper.

Grind the nuts and dates in a food processor or fine mincer. Bring the water to the boil and stir in the nut mixture and sugar. Blend the ground rice with the milk and add to the nut mixture. Bring back to the boil, stirring, and cook for 2 minutes until thickened.

Spoon into a warmed serving dish, decorate with an apple flower and serve hot.

▓ COOK'S TIP

Agar-agar is an extremely useful setting agent which has no flavour of its own and does not require refrigeration. Because the results are rather stiffer than those achieved with gelatine, a contrasting coolness and softness is provided by the fruit.

▓ COOK'S TIP

To make an apple flower, thinly pare the peel from a small hard green apple, taking care to keep it in one piece. Curl the peel into a tight circle to make a flower.

235 CHINESE FRUIT SALAD

Preparation time:
20-25 minutes, plus
chilling

Serves 4

Calories:
100-200 per portion

YOU WILL NEED:
1 large honeydew melon
4-5 types fresh or canned fruit, with
the syrup from one can (see
Cook's Tip)

Cut the honeydew melon in half and scoop out and discard the seeds. Cut the flesh into small chunks and reserve the shell.

Prepare the remaining fruit according to type. Leave small fruits whole if appropriate, otherwise cut into chunks the same size as the melon.

Mix the melon pieces with the fruit and syrup from the can. Pack the melon shell with this mixture, then cover tightly with clingfilm. Chill for at least 2 hours in the refrigerator before serving.

236 EIGHT-TREASURE RICE PUDDING

Preparation time:
20 minutes

Cooking time:
1¼ -1½ hours

Serves 6

Calories:
550 per portiron

YOU WILL NEED:
350 g/12 oz pudding rice
4 tablespoons caster sugar
50 g/2 oz unsalted butter
100 g/4 oz glacé cherries, chopped
50 g/2 oz crystallized orange peel,
chopped
25 g/1 oz each angelica, walnuts
and blanched almonds, chopped
50 g/2 oz seedless raisins, chopped
5 tablespoons sweet red bean paste
300 ml/ ½ pint syrup (see Cook's Tip)

Rinse the rice, drain and put in a pan with enough water to cover. Simmer for 15 minutes, drain, and stir in the sugar and half the butter.

Use the remaining butter to grease a 900-ml/1½ pint pudding basin, then line with a thin layer of rice. Press a little of each fruit and nut into this to make a decorative patttern. Mix the remaining rice, fruit and nuts together. Spoon alternate layers of this rice mixture and bean paste into the basin, finishing with a layer of rice. Press down firmly. Cover with greaseproof paper and pleated foil and steam for 1-1¼ hours.

Turn the pudding out on to a serving dish and serve hot with the warm syrup.

▒ COOK'S TIP

For the assorted fruits,
choose from bananas, grapes,
kiwi fruit, lychees, guavas,
mangoes and peaches or
nectarines. Try to include at
least 4 types of fruit.

▒ COOK'S TIP

To make the syrup for this
recipe, add 50 g/2 oz sugar to
300 ml/ ½ pint water and
bring to the boil, stirring
constantly to dissolve the
sugar. Remove from the heat

and add a few drops of
almond essence, vanilla
essence, rose water or
orange-flower water. Pour
over the pudding and serve
hot.

INDEX